REBOOT

[REBOOT]

COMPETING WITH TECHNOLOGY STRATEGY

LISA B. JASPER AND JIM SMELLEY

INSPIRE™
ON PURPOSE
Bringing Inspiration to Print

Graphic illustrations by Jennifer Carter
Cover design by Josh Surgeon

Disclaimer: The advice and strategies contained herein may not be suitable for every situation. This work is sold with the understanding that the publisher is not engaged in rendering legal, accounting, or other professional services. If professional assistance is required, the services of a competent professional should be sought. Neither the publisher nor the authors shall be liable for damages arising from use or misuse of this information.

Published by Inspire On Purpose™
909 Lake Carolyn Parkway, Suite 300
Irving, Texas 75039
Toll Free 888-403-2727
www.inspireonpurpose.com
The Platform Publisher™

INSPIRE™
ON PURPOSE
Bringing Inspiration to Print

Printed in the United States of America
Library of Congress Control Number: 2011931545
ISBN 10: 0982562209
ISBN 13: 9780982562208

To Meich and Peich and Mom and Dad

Acknowledgments

Our sincere thanks to…

Our colleagues at Thought Ensemble: John, who makes sure every client is happy; Claudia, who somehow keeps the engine running; and Anthony, whose energy and inspiration keeps us moving forward. You make our company great.

Our publishing team, Terri and Michelle at Inspire on Purpose. You took on this book like it was your own. You helped us keep it real and weave our ideas together. Our readers will thank you, too!

All the mentors, guides, and teachers who inspired us along the way as we've explored the ideas that provided a foundation for this book. There are too many to list but a few that stand out include Brian, Bruce, Katherine, Linda, Rene, Russ, Lori, Patrick, Scott, and Saurajit.

George and Eric, for your patience and support through this entire endeavor.

Our families who brought us up in a world of possibilities—you taught us the value of continuous learning and the push for mastery.

CONTENTS

Acknowledgments   vii

Introduction: *No Time for Conventionality*   1

Section 1   An Unfair Fight

1   The Great Divide: *How Goliath Grew Two Heads*   5

2   Armed and Dangerous: *David Has a New Set of Tools*   19

Section 2   A New Twist on Technology Strategy

3   The MAP Guided Tour: *Lemons Into Lemonade*   31

4   Model: *Organizing Thought*   49

5   Approach: *Science as a Competitive Weapon*   73

6   Project: *The Road to Reboot*   87

Section 3   Press the Reboot Button

7   Monday Morning: *A Fresh Start*   105

About the Authors   113

About the Comics   115

INTRODUCTION
NO TIME FOR
CONVENTIONALITY

Let's break ground with a short history of the ancient past.

It all began in 1995. Okay, that may not seem exactly like the "ancient past," but for this book, it is essentially the point of origin. It was during this time that the World Wide Web spidered out from its inception in academia and military research. And since this book is primarily about once-geeky stuff, like how information technology has changed and is still changing the way business is conducted, 1995 is a critical milestone.

It also happens to be the year that we (the authors) graduated from college. We had nerdy degrees in a time before nerds acquired the ironically cool image they now enjoy. (Damn you, lucky young nerds!) We took nerdy jobs as the "tech people" at two big professional services companies. We worked on some of the biggest system implementations ever attempted. It was a fascinating vantage point from which to watch businesses evolve as the Internet spread. We've been watching this evolution (and sometimes been fortunate enough to be involved) throughout our careers.

But don't worry. This isn't a history book or a memoir of two nerds. This is a practical, how-to book. It's a how-to book on an important subject: namely how to create strategy in a business world rapidly changing as a result of technology innovation. This book offers a means of increasing your company's ability to compete by thinking about technology differently.

We're going to argue that technology is a central component of business strategy today. That is what we believe. No matter what Nicholas Carr said. No matter what your CFO thinks, and yes, regardless of what your CEO says. If they don't recognize that this once-nerdy technology stuff is now a central component of business strategy, they are wrong, and your company is in trouble. More than any other trend today, technology continues to remake businesses and industries as new competitors and entire industries quickly rise to supplant their ancestors.

It was common in the 1990s to talk about how technology would "change everything." Then, the double financial busts of the first decade of the 2000s drew attention from the changes underway. Despite the busts, technology continued to evolve and businesses invested heavily. Those businesses that embraced technology from a revolutionary vantage point are now the companies we admire. Why? They used innovation to compete their way to the top. They did it better and faster.

We will argue that most organizations get this technology strategy stuff horribly wrong—that they are using an antiquated model for thinking about technology and that this accounts for many of the casualties that litter the business world.

Finally, we will argue that there is a better way to think strategically about technology and a better way to deliver on it. We call it the Strategy MAP. Okay, it's a cheesy name, but it could be worse. Our publisher wanted us to re-order the letters to create the "Strategy AMP: Boosting your strategy to the next phase." Her advice is usually spot on, but that was too much, even for us nerds.

Clever acronyms aside, the Strategy MAP solution we propose in this book is grounded in something pretty venerable: science. No, we're not talking about some weird middle school science laboratory. The scientific approach is simply a way of thinking about problems and opportunities and testing solutions the way modern scientists do.

We realize that science isn't the most traveled path for people seeking ideas for business thinking. Based on the offerings in our local Barnes and Noble, businesspeople prefer lessons and metaphors from war, psychology, religion, or engineering. Science-based books don't seem to land on the business shelves very often. Yet, the approach to "thought" promoted by science is particularly valuable in the case of technology because technology now enables businesses to launch and test experiments faster and cheaper than ever before. Advancements in modern technology make the basic scientific approach for designing a business hypothesis, rapidly creating an experiment, and quickly testing that experiment in the market, much easier than it once was.

We're not attempting to be the last word on strategy, much less technology strategy. This isn't the kind of book that bombastically reveals the secrets to a successful business in four easy steps. This book is simply part of the conversation on how technology has changed business and what to do about it. We are sharing an approach that we have found helpful—one that we think might help you, too.

However, it first requires one big leap across the Great Divide.

SECTION 1

AN UNFAIR FIGHT

CHAPTER 1

THE GREAT DIVIDE

HOW GOLIATH
GREW TWO HEADS

How did once powerful businesses lose to smaller, faster companies who innovated their way to the top? How did so many businesses cede the high ground on technology leadership?

The truth is most businesses are not organized to deliver technology in a strategic way. If you work in or near an information technology (IT) organization, this won't come as a surprise. The traditional divided structure where IT is a separate group from the rest of the company may be effective for managing cost and reducing risk, but it isn't effective at enabling companies to be more competitive through technology. Please don't be offended if you work in an excellent IT shop. We know you guys are out there, but you are a rare few.

Of all the organizations found within a company, IT is often the least liked and respected. Worse yet, IT employees, despite being some of the most highly paid, are often the least happy and, consequently, the most likely to leave. These internal IT organizations are rarely innovative. Their role has basically been relegated to glorified order takers responding to requests from the rest of the organization, which people in IT refer to as "the business" (as if people in IT somehow are not part of "the business" themselves). Then, there are those supposedly forward-thinking organizations that refer to business units as the "customer" (as if they have forgotten who the real customer of the organization is). We just don't get it. IT *is* part of the business, and the entire business succeeds only when it serves the ultimate end-user customer.

This problem hit home recently when we started working with a new client and had the unusual opportunity to listen to some recent audio recordings of interviews with their executive team, done by another consulting firm. From what we heard, this firm had been asked to help fix the relationship between the client's IT organization and its business executives, but had made the problem worse.

As soon as we listened to these interviews, we realized why. The consulting firm's perspective was so far off the mark that the interviewees were hopelessly frustrated just by the questions asked. Yet we almost couldn't blame the consulting firm—the questions asked were actually quite typical of the language used around IT today. What was atypical were the executives' responses.

Here's a snippet of one of the conversations:

Interviewer:
Let's start with an open-ended question. How well do you think your IT organization is serving you?

Client Executive (you can almost hear him frowning):
You see, that is the problem right there. You've got the wrong perspective. They shouldn't be trying to serve me. They should be trying to create value for our customers.

Interviewer:
Fair enough. But how well is IT meeting the needs of your business to help you create value for your customers?

Client Executive:
Look, I don't think you realize just how bad this has gotten here. Do you know that the people in IT now go through "Customer Service" training? And guess who the "customer" is? *ME!* That is absolutely ridiculous.

Interviewer:
Sure, we see this disconnect all the time, but it doesn't appear to be much worse here than anywhere else. They are just trying to run their IT organization like a business. You actually have a fairly efficient IT organization.

Client Executive (clearly exasperated):
Efficient yes, but I don't think you understand. Last year, our former CIO requested funding for a Customer Relationship Management system to track *internal* customers. Let's just think about how perverse that is. We don't even have a functioning CRM to allow us to share information across our business about our *external* customers (sighing).

Things are different now. A few years ago, we could afford to delay our investment in technology. In fact, we encouraged it. We were burned by excessive spending in the 1990s and had too many failed projects. We figured that if we were slow to spend in IT, we would make fewer mistakes. So we decided to become "deliberate." But that isn't working either. I can't quite put my finger on it. I'm not a technology expert. Our traditional big competitors are still slow (thank God), but you wouldn't believe how quickly new small guys are entering our space. Just this morning, we lost a huge piece of business from our biggest client to a new company that has been around for *less than six months*. We've been in this business for over 100 years, and we're losing to some kids in a garage. Using technology strategically isn't an academic exercise for us. It is life or death.

The executive made two key points in this conversation. First, he pointed out that his IT organization was focused on the wrong thing: their internal customers. Second, he pointed out the related consequence: that his company was missing opportunities to use technology as a competitive weapon. While he couldn't quite put his finger on what had gone wrong, he nailed the problem. His IT organization's internal focus was distracting from real opportunities.

So how did we, business and IT, get here? How is it that corporations spun one of the most important competitive weapons in the modern business arsenal into an insignificant tool? And the people? How did we arrive at a divided IT group that is frequently disliked, underperforming and often unhappy? When did innovation become drudgery? *What happened to IT?*

Don't get us wrong—despite the absence of strategic leveraging of IT in most companies, technology has still revolutionized the business world. Here are a few highlights:

- The entire music industry was remade in less than ten years.
- The television and movie industry are in the middle of radical change now, as Internet-powered video transforms the business models of cable and satellite providers.
- Printed newspapers are disappearing quickly as the Web and digital readers steal the audience, and only specialized print publications appear poised to survive.

But wait, there's more:

- Car companies are competing by embedding more technology in their dashboards.
- Banks have moved most low-value transactions to computers.
- Legal transactions are now handled by digital platforms delivered "in the cloud" with low-paid customer service agents serving the customer rather than lawyers (bad news for recent law school grads).
- Energy companies use increasingly sophisticated computer systems to find oil, and computers even control the processing and distribution of oil once it's out of the ground.
- Charities take donations via text message. Think about that for a second—donations by text messages.

Additionally, the increasing push toward globalization (which many claim is the most important business trend) is largely underpinned by technology. Email and file sharing were the first critical Internet-enabled activities. Now, these and more advanced collaboration tools make working with global teams not only easier, but more effective. Inside even the most staid, old-fashioned industries, technology is taking an increasingly prominent role, as it improves the productivity of workers across geographies and increases the analytic and decision-making capabilities of the entire organization.

The strategic role of technology and the ability to manage it successfully are not commonly understood disciplines. It is no wonder. The seminal works of business strategy were largely written before technology really became a central component of business strategy. Porter, Drucker, and Hammer all wrote their most widely known and commonly studied works well before technology accelerated the ability to compete. These excellent books are largely silent on the issues of technology, and the few that address it at all are naive about the issues that face twenty-first century businesses.

Walk into any bookstore (assuming you still go to a bookstore in person), and you'll find shelves littered with books on implementing and measuring business strategy. These books rarely touch on the strategic importance of technology.

Additionally, countless volumes dive deep into technical concepts, programming languages, and project management. Some even make an effort to explore technology strategy. Many of these books offer good ideas and frameworks, but almost universally, they approach the topic from inside an IT organization or inside existing technology. They frequently miss the competitive advantage that a company (or industry for that matter) can wield when technology is applied strategically.

And it doesn't stop there. The other places companies go to for advice—other publications, advisory and consulting firms—also miss this critical topic.

With this gap in strategic thinking, most organizations are left to fend for themselves and consequently, "wing it" when building technology strategies. Too often this leaves the strategic process without real fuel within the organization, leading companies to create middling, ineffective strategies, or more often, a series of disconnected initiatives with little holding them together.

This book is a call to "reboot"—to rethink the way businesses strategically work *with* technology. It is designed to spark thinking and encourage insight. It is written to hearten those who work with technology (there is more to success in IT than simple preoccupation with lowering costs or increasing responsiveness), and it is meant to encourage those in the rest of the organization who yearn for clear ways of thinking about technology. We hope it is a kick in the pants for those who are stuck, and a call to arms for the next generation of nerds who are tasked with making sense of the tangle of technology.

We need to reboot many of the old ideas and start afresh.

But first, let's examine how we got those "old ideas."

A Brief History of Technology — With a New Lens

To understand how we got to this unfortunate situation, a brief history of technology in business is in order. We'll talk about how IT and business divided over the last fifty years into a two-headed Goliath. We all know what happens in the conflict between David and Goliath, but a *two-headed* Goliath adds a new twist to the story. This Goliath is big, slow, strong, *and* schizophrenic. In this chapter, we'll discover how this two-headed Goliath formed and strengthened over these years.

A word to you fellow nerds: Those of you who are familiar with the history of technology within organizations because you've read about it or lived through it may be tempted to skip this section or just skim it. We wholeheartedly support that approach. If you want to skim through, just look for the parts about how Goliath's second head sprouted, grew and solidified through each major technology wave. That evolution is the key takeaway of this chapter. Hopefully we didn't spoil it for the rest of you!

Believe it or not, computers only entered the business world about fifty years ago. While it is a somewhat arbitrary date, we will start around 1960 as we assess the effect of information technology on modern commerce. By 1960, about 6,000 computers were operating in the U.S., but it was largely government and research institutions that used these machines. For example, computers had been used to process the 1950 census, predict the election of Dwight D. Eisenhower (1952), and photocopy paper (1959). But until the 1960s, they hadn't moved significantly into the business world.

In 1960, American Airlines launched a major investment in technology called SABRE. American Airlines was growing rapidly, but this growth presented its own challenges. The company was

overwhelmed with slow, manual, error-prone processes, particularly in processing new reservations, responding to customer requests and managing the many operational issues that airlines face (e.g., weather delays, maintenance, ground control, etc.).

American Airlines had already made attempts at rudimentary solutions involving early computers when the president, C.R. Smith, sat down on a flight next to an IBM sales rep (at least, this is how the story is widely told). They began talking and realized that some of the experimental systems that IBM had been building for the military could be repurposed for use at the airline. This happenstance discussion launched a project that eventually created SABRE, which originally stood for Semi-Automated Business Research Environment. SABRE went "live" as a prototype in 1960. If a time machine is ever invented, we'd like to travel back to the day when C.R. Smith sold this idea to his board. (Did anyone ask him to fill out the standard business case template? Probably not.)

SABRE, one of the first major applications built in any business, gave American Airlines a strategic cost and information advantage over its competitors that lasted decades. This one move allowed American Airlines to leapfrog its competition. It gave the company a combined reservation and scheduling system, as SABRE handled the challenges of running reservations in a global airline. It also allowed American to price and re-price faster and with fewer resources than its non-computer-enabled competitors. In fact, SABRE was so far ahead of the competition that many of their competitors paid American to use the system rather than struggle to catch American's lead.

Another benefit for American was that having its competition on its own system increased American's information advantage over the rest of the industry. American knew what its competition was doing, and better yet, what its competition's customers were doing.

Around this same time, a few other companies began to successfully implement game-changing systems. Then in 1963, Digital Equipment Corporation launched the first successful minicomputer. Originally seen as toys by many of the people working on mainframes—foreshadowing the same comments later made about PCs and mobile phones—the lower cost of minicomputers and easier programming languages (COBOL in 1959 and BASIC in 1964) enabled even more businesses to explore the information technology frontier. By 1975, more than 5,000 minicomputers had been sold in the U.S.

The technology wave continued to gain momentum in the business world, and by the late 1970s, most businesses of any size had computers performing basic tasks. In addition to accounting, bill printing, and reservations, computers were used for payroll, operations, and manufacturing. These were still massive systems tackling big problems, tightly managed by a small, select group of technologists who researched the problem, built the software, and decided who could use what and when.

So, if you can accept that 1960 is the starting date for the use of computers in business, that means we have just over fifty years of experience with them. Although we've learned a great deal in the past five decades, that isn't a lot of time to really learn how to use a new kind of technology. Is it any surprise we have not yet learned the best way to organize technology investments or build technology solutions, much less the best way to *think* about technology?

Let's get back to the birth of the Great Divide between IT and business people and the creation of the two-headed Goliath. Up until the mid-1970s, the IT people within businesses were still a relatively small group and closely tied to business needs. But that was about to change.

Personal Computers

The next wave of infiltration by computers took a different path and involved a completely different set of people. The personal computer (PC) was born in 1975 when Altair released the Altair 8800. Then in 1977, Apple introduced the prototype of a fully assembled computer, the Apple II. For the first time, information technology innovation broke through the size and cost barrier that had locked it inside only large institutions. Initially, the PC inched its way into households and schools where people began interacting directly with computers mostly as a substitute for the typewriter or as a device on which to play games. For most, this was the first time they personally laid a hand on a computer. Consumers were fascinated, despite how little those early gems actually did.

During the 1980s, the PC began invading corporations, frequently bypassing the IT group who thought of them once again as toys (an attitude reinforced by the sales and marketing arms of the companies who manufactured the expensive and profitable mainframes and minicomputers). On the eve of the greatest evolutionary leap since the Industrial Revolution, the tech people in many businesses resisted the PC as if it were an invader and built bulwarks against its infiltration into their enterprise.

Despite the resistance, the powerful, portable PC soon spread to more kinds of businesses and into more corners within companies. In a few short years, the PC started to appear on almost every desk and to be used for a host of new functions: data analysis, faxing, spreadsheets, information organization, communication, presentations, and personal productivity.

Although initially sluggish to adopt the PC, tech people reversed course and took on the challenge of writing the new kinds of software made possible by PCs. These applications, fueled by a host of newer, easier programming languages, and prebuilt software packages, furthered the surge of software that poured into businesses.

For the first time, however, computers that showed up on corporate desktops could not be completely controlled by the IT staff. With PCs, the user was in control. Data could be transferred on the new fancy floppy disks from user to user. Executives and employees could even create their own rudimentary applications without the help of people in the tech group. In a foreshadowing of what is happening today, technology in businesses began to diverge from the immediate control of the organizational hierarchy; and as it diverged, strategic thinking about technology began to split as well.

Most business people were not yet aware of the strategic importance of technology. Executives were primarily concerned about larger and larger technology spending—budgets were out of control, and the root cause was the ubiquitous PC.

The reaction of the business community was predictable: insert more control, more hierarchy, and more process. And the IT organization was needed to manage it all. This is when Goliath sprouted a second head.

Email and the Internet

The next major wave of innovation wasn't hardware related. It was a single application—email. Email lodged itself into businesses by capitalizing on a new network of networks: the Internet. Although email had existed since the 1960s or 1970s (depending on what start date you want to use for an actual "mail" system on a computer), it didn't become widespread until the mid- to late-1980s. As the technology spread into more and more companies, *not* having email was a liability. The speed and efficiency it enabled in communication was addictive.

As with the tools that preceded it, email remade entire business functions. Instant, written communication reached multiple people at the same time, allowed written records of conversations, and sped up response time. Email had huge advantages over the three dominant internal communication mechanisms of the past: printed memos (could reach many people, but were slow), telephones (faster, but could only connect to one person), and meetings (could reach many people, but were costly and time-consuming as well as difficult to arrange before email facilitated the scheduling process). Again, in a remarkably small timespan, a new technology reshaped businesses. The printed memo all but disappeared, and the telephone ceased to be the primary mode of communication in most businesses. The only remaining vestige of pre-information technology communication is the meeting—and as we'll see in the next chapter, even that is being transformed.

Businesses adopted email at a rapid pace, at first dominantly for internal communication, and then for communicating with people outside the organization as well: suppliers, customers, competitors, bankers, lawyers, and regulators. The advantages email brought to internal communication were magnified in external communication. Email was much more efficient and effective than trying to reach someone outside the company using traditional methods like phone calls, faxes, or meetings. The computer kept a record of all correspondence, and multiple people could receive and respond to the same message at the same time. This application signaled one of the most important (but not obvious at the time) capabilities of technology—it could connect people in ways never before imagined.

At the same time, as businesses began using email to connect to the businesses around them, they were not only improving their interactions and speeding up the whole world of commerce; they were also exposing their companies to new risks. Data was easy to transfer via email, and businesses began to see one of the most crucial strategic issues that would arise from the increasing use of technology: security.

Email was mission-critical *and risky.* And businesses reacted in a logical way at the time. If they didn't already have a separate IT group, they created one. If they had a separate IT group, they gave it additional power. Organizational lines and hierarchy were strengthened as the IT group began to be seen as a separate part of the company. Especially in large organizations, this division became much clearer. Goliath's second head began to take shape.

The World Wide Web

The World Wide Web was another application built on the back of the Internet that began to emerge around 1995. This technology solidified the divided role of IT in most businesses, and continued to develop Goliath's second head.

At first, most businesses saw the effect of the Web as trivial, less important than email. In fact, many ignored it for years. Even when they finally began addressing the Web, they weren't sure what to do with it. Companies initially thought of the Web as simply another place to put their brochures, leading to a common 1990s term: "brochure-ware." The first corporate Web "sites" provided little more than an overview of the company, essential product information, maybe some flattering pictures of the executives and basic contact information. Unfortunately, many websites still look like that today. Even though these first paltry attempts didn't seem like a revolution, the technology underlying the Internet, on which the World Wide Web was built, enabled a remarkable advance in creativity for those who recognized it. Evolution became a revolution, even if many businesses missed it.

As innovators pushed new ideas and business models onto the Web, many businesses that had done well for decades or even centuries were crippled, or at best, handcuffed. The Web spread quickly, and by the last five years of the 1990s, a handful of new and successful ventures powered by the Web had become household names, including Amazon, eBay, Yahoo! and AOL.

These companies were led by cutting-edge explorers who ventured into this unknown territory to claim their space. In fact, the dominant metaphors of the time were geography based: "sites" were "under construction," users "visited" different "addresses" on the Web and travelled an "Internet Superhighway" that connected it all. Like adventurous explorers, early tech pioneers made remarkable progress considering how unclear the territory was at the time. These were the winners. They were the scientists who remained true to their experimental tests of technology.

And there were losers. For every company that was successful in this new Web world, dozens (perhaps hundreds) failed. Not only did startups trying to claim territory in the new world fail, but so did businesses that had been around for decades. Bookstores, record labels, airlines, encyclopedias, hotel chains, retail outlets, newspapers, phonebook printers, travel agents, Realtors, and many other businesses that were too slow to realize what was going on began to lose their customers and their profits.

Sony could have created Napster or iTunes, but it didn't. Barnes and Noble could have created Amazon; AT&T could have created Google; Britannica could have created Wikipedia, or the *Chicago Tribune* could have created eBay or Craigslist; but they didn't.

None of these older businesses had a winning strategy for using new technology. The two-headed Goliath that had emerged as the dominant way of organizing technology investment contributed substantially to this problem. One head looked at the other and said, "You are the IT guys; you figure out what we should do about this Web thing." The other head looked back and said, "You are the business guys, you tell us what you want to do, and we'll make it happen." As you might expect, a two-headed Goliath was even slower than his one-headed predecessor.

The Technology Strategy Gap

Goliath businesses missed many opportunities. The latter half of the twentieth century saw immense and successive waves of change brought on by technological forces, and at an increasingly faster pace. Existing businesses struggled while aggressive upstarts gained ground. New businesses took risks, envisioned new products powered by innovative technologies, saw weaknesses in the competition, conducted experiments, and—with a momentum and drive that few of their large competitors could match—created the dominant technology platforms and businesses of the new world.

Goliath businesses struggled. If they were the dominant force in the business world before, in the new age, they were sluggish, impotent, and appallingly unable to respond to the changes around them. Confronted each day by the challenges of the present, many businesses failed to distinguish the trivial from the significant and the tactical from the strategic. The development of IT strategy and business strategy as two separate heads was a core part of the problem. Instead of two heads being better than one, companies became of two minds, and were often pulled in two different directions when trying to think strategically.

CIOs and various consulting firms began to try to patch up Goliath and his two heads using a variety of catch-phrase approaches that you might remember.

Failed Two-Headed Goliath Fix #1: Alignment

The first approach to the two-headed Goliath problem was called *alignment*. CIOs and other technology leaders pursued this indistinct goal for years. The major research and analysis companies studied the alignment issue, which frequently appeared as the top concern of CIOs in industry surveys through the 1990s and beyond. Yet, the concept was difficult to define, hard to act on, and impossible to achieve with certainty.

The strategy was sometimes couched as "being responsive to customers"—a concept even worse than the idea of alignment because it advocated thinking of the company as a customer and thus created a pseudo-market within the organization. Talking about other people inside the organization as if they were the customers was a distraction from the real work of technology strategy and soon became a blind alley for many organizations.

By this point in technology history, the Web and supporting technologies were so transformative that simply doing whatever the guys on the top floor said to do was a woefully lacking response to the challenges and opportunities presented by new technology. Businesses and their IT organizations simply couldn't keep up with the rapidly changing competitive landscape, and their failure to do so left an opening for external service providers to step in with proposed solutions and lure away the attention (and dollars) of business executives.

Failed Two-Headed Goliath Fix #2: IT Isn't Strategic

In the early part of the 2000s, pundits tried other ways of tackling the two-headed Goliath problem. First, they tried to minimize the strategic importance of technology, basically saying that there was no strategic value to technology, so just don't worry about it.

This idea was easy to sell because IT strategies were failing left and right inside most companies. Weary business executives reflexively flocked around pundits who proclaimed the view that IT was not a strategic investment because they had been burned by excessive spending on unjustified and non-strategic technology during the first wave of excitement around the Web. This wet blanket spread over business thinking and into IT department culture, and it has dampened strategic thinking about technology in many organizations to this day.

Business leaders found false comfort in this thought. If IT isn't strategic, it doesn't require our attention, and we can forget about it. At the same time, CIOs and IT department heads tried to protect their jobs as the CFO whittled away budgets and the rest of the C-suite unknowingly stifled innovation. Any notion of experimentation with new technology was extinguished. IT wasn't strategic—or so they said.

Failed Two-Headed Goliath Fix #3: The Trusted Advisor

Meanwhile, other IT organizations were trying to achieve the elusive "Trusted Advisor" status. Although the concept of alignment was still hot, it was clearly not achieving its grand vision of unlocking "the potential of IT" inside organizations. CIOs wanted to go beyond alignment. The new buzz centered on being a Trusted Advisor. The Holy Grail for the CIO was getting a seat at the proverbial table—the C-suite or boardroom table—so that the CIO could advise business executives on how technology could improve their company and its revenues.

But the Trusted Advisor approach does little to close the gap between the business people and the IT people. In fact, it exacerbates the problem because it reinforces the idea that there is a separate business that needs advice on technology, and that this separate group needs to simply "trust" the technology team. This model may work well for external consultants and other service providers, but it is a dead end for the internal development of technology strategies.

Failed Two-Headed Goliath Fix #4: Running IT Like a Business

In a desperate attempt to find a way to make the two-headed Goliath work, many businesses decided to run the IT organization as if it were a separate business—and in doing so, only strengthened the division between the business people and the IT people. Promoted by consulting companies and industry gurus with books like *Managing IT as a Business* by Mark Lutchen or *The Real Business of IT* by Richard Hunter and George Westerman, this idea seeped into much of the language inside businesses and IT organizations. Technology people frequently talk about other people in the organization as their *customers* or *clients*. They talk about *selling* projects to the organization. Some even built internal sales systems to track the "selling" process of projects through the organization. Others tried to transform themselves from a cost center to a generator of financial results.

This way of thinking (which is the dominant approach in many businesses as we write this book) is doing nothing more than strengthening the two-headed Goliath. It reinforces the damaging idea that two kinds of people exist inside organizations: business people and technology people. It creates confusion about who the real customers of the organization are—the people or organizations that pay money for its products, not other people *inside* the organization. It creates bad

relationships within the organization because the people within the organization don't want to be sold. They don't want to be "relationship managed." They don't want to be manipulated or treated like targets from which the IT department can extract more money.

This divide between technology people and business people inside the organization has become so entrenched, and the gap so wide, that very little technology strategy occurs in most businesses. IT organizations that try to "run like a business" usually focus by default on cost reduction, which simply accelerates the commoditization of the applications and services provided by the company. Cost reduction itself is not a bad idea, but it does nothing to distinguish the organization or differentiate it from its competition. This focus on cost reduction has stripped the technology capabilities of many businesses at exactly the same time new innovators are investing and taking an experimental and innovative approach to technology.

By focusing almost exclusively on reducing costs or simply being "responsive" to "the business," many IT organizations—and therefore many businesses—have lost the vision and vigor necessary to act strategically and have suffocated innovation within their walls. All the while, external innovation speeds up and new competitors use technology to undercut existing businesses. David is taking down Goliath right before our eyes.

Now that we've taken a trip down Memory Lane and rekindled your desire to change the world, we want to invite you to get a new set of tools: competitive weaponry.

In the next chapter, we will talk about David and the new tools available to him—and to you—even as our two-headed Goliath argues with himself.

CHAPTER 2

ARMED AND DANGEROUS

DAVID HAS A
NEW SET OF TOOLS

The social and digital evolution is changing the business world almost daily. "Speed" is no longer simply an argument about the benefits of getting to market faster versus other benefits (higher quality, lower cost). Speed is suddenly a basic requirement to compete. Daily technology advances appear to take shape literally on top of each other, and all of it occurs at an increasingly faster pace.

Case in point: The iPad went from a predicted loser to a must-have deployment vehicle for all sorts of industries in less than *six months.* It was followed by dozens of competitors, virtually overnight. Now, there are two iPads and all kinds of other tablets everywhere. And people have already built hundreds of thousands of applications for them, creating new forms of interaction, thought, and more important, new methods of commerce.

The capabilities of the newest advances in technology are changing competition by making it easier for David to start a company. They enable small companies to have many of the technology capabilities of much larger corporations. They make David's start-up look bigger from day one. They make it easier to innovate, and they make it easier to be fast. However, as we'll explore in the coming chapters, Goliath businesses can take advantage of these new technologies with as much speed and determination as the small guys; it just takes a change in thinking—a reboot in mind-set.

But back to David. David has gained a new set of powerful tools that enable him to compete more fiercely and more quickly. Three current tools are particularly interesting from this viewpoint of competitive weaponry: the rising use of mobile devices, using the Internet as a platform, and the emerging collaboration and sharing of applications on the Web.

More interesting than their introduction alone, these three creative technologies are simultaneously feeding off of each other. Advances in one area are immediately leveraged in another with stunning eagerness. Today, Google announces a new search product. Tomorrow, someone will start building a new business idea on top of it. In a month or two, that business could be live and fully functional, taking down another Goliath.

The question we should be asking ourselves is, "How can I capitalize on these three innovative trends to enhance my company's ability to compete, or to revolutionize our product set, or better yet, to create a new industry?"

Talking about these technological advances is not a new concept. You've probably already read theories about all three. Rather than pose theories, we invite you to think about innovation in the midst of these changes. How can your company think differently about these new advances rather than simply react to them?

Depending on what kind of organization you are in, you may or may not have personally resonated with the challenges of a two-headed Goliath. (If you didn't, consider yourself one of the lucky few.) But, no matter your business, these trends will affect you. So as you read this chapter, think about what your strategy is to leverage each of these technological advances. Consider where your competitors are, where you may have missed opportunities, and what opportunities are out there to exploit.

Technological Shift #1: Mobile Devices

Mobile computing has been around for several decades, but mobile devices (and the utility infrastructure behind them) have only recently evolved to the point where they are disrupting business strategies.

As computing power gets smaller and cheaper every year, the devices get smaller and more powerful. Obviously this is an influential, if not critical, factor at play in the competitive marketplace. Humans are mobile beings who want to stay connected. And since we're already mobile, we might as well be productive, right?

Much like during the personal computer era, businesses (who should know better by now) are slow to adopt mobile innovation even though data-capable devices are now in the hands of most of their employees and customers. At best, companies view these devices only as a phone or email device. At worst, they view these devices as "toys" or solely tools for personal use. Neither viewpoint empowers competitive thought or the ability to create new ways of selling, marketing, communicating and collaborating with customers.

Think about it. How does the technological ability to text donations to a nonprofit change the way a business could compete? And, how did this application first get implemented within the nonprofit sector before a Goliath brand used it to increase profits through mobile sales of its products?

And now that iTunes has revolutionized the distribution of software applications, are sales and marketing departments at Goliath companies breaking down the proverbial walls of the IT department to create and test new hypotheses about this mobile distribution system, or are they simply watching as start-ups beat them to it?

These mobile devices create a bond between companies and their mobile customers and provide David with his first set of tools in the new social/digital decade. Mobile devices are no longer simply telephones. Right before this book went to print, data traffic outpaced voice traffic for the first time in history. Nor are they simply devices to text or view email, although that is precisely how most Goliath companies are viewing them.

The vast stores of data and processing power of the Internet have multiplied mobile capabilities. Supercharged mobile devices have already changed the way consumers meet new people, find places

to eat and shop, identify and purchase music, check movie reviews, buy stocks, check the weather, find traffic information, keep up with friends, arrange meetings, date, plan trips, settle bar bets, check email, access news, read books, conduct research, count calories, comparison shop, entertain and educate themselves, take/view/share pictures, watch TV, work and so many other things we could take up the entire book just listing them. If your mobile customers cannot connect with you, then clearly, it is time to find a new way to think and act about technology in your business.

Not only is innovation in mobile devices and software occurring at a blistering pace, but the speed of consumer adoption is mind-blowing. Hence, any business that wants to compete effectively will have to adopt equally as fast, if not ahead of the consumer. Many experts predict that within ten years the price of mobile devices will be so low and the availability so ubiquitous that practically anyone on the planet who wants an Internet-enabled mobile device will have one. That means the pressure and competition is on, not just locally, but globally. No business can afford to wait to develop a technology strategy that enables them to compete quickly and effectively in this ever-expanding marketplace.

Creative, forward-thinking companies are thriving amid the chaos in this space. The fast innovation, the destruction of value in old sectors and the creation of value in new ones are heralding the rapid end of profit models that existed for decades.

So the question is: *What is your company doing about mobility?* Are you reacting, or are you experimenting with a new hypothesis about how customers will use this technology? What is your company doing right now to leverage mobile technology? Are you simply making your website viewable from a mobile device (which is what most companies are doing), or are you thinking like your customer and rethinking how they might interact with your company from a mobile device?

Yes, David has a new set of tools. And Goliath will be crippled if he can't learn how to think differently about the mobility of customers and how to leverage technology to engage with customers where they are, even when they're on the go.

Technological Shift #2: The Internet as Platform (a.k.a. "The Cloud")

The Internet may sound like an old piece of technology to some, but businesses are building new things on top of this network-of-networks every day. This "platform" is getting stronger, more robust and faster every year—so fast that many companies cannot possibly keep pace. As you probably know, these Internet as a Platform services fall mainly into two (albeit not completely distinct) categories with appropriately fancy and sexy buzzwords: Software as a Service (SaaS) and Utility Computing. Many refer to this overall set of services with an even fancier and sexier buzzword: "The Cloud."

Technological Shift #2A: SaaS (Software as a Service)

The first Internet as a Platform innovation is Software as a Service. SaaS is basically a method of providing software over the Internet so that companies can use it without a long-term commitment, hardware installation, or ongoing system maintenance. Building and maintaining software is expensive, so until now, having infrastructure gave Goliath a strategic advantage, because David couldn't afford to compete. Ironically, what was once an advantage—being able to afford systems and infrastructure—is now one of Goliath's major weaknesses. Technology can change so rapidly that owning infrastructure can now be a competitive disadvantage, because that infrastructure is what often impedes a company's ability to react quickly.

The list of benefits for businesses leveraging SaaS is pretty long. They no longer have to invest in additional technology infrastructure. They can more readily scale up or down. They can maximize the value of someone else's innovation, etc. These innovations put technology tools that were previously reserved for the largest companies with deep pockets into the hands of small operations. Some call it the democratization of software, and it is empowering small businesses. Not only does David have new tools, but he has a speed advantage too.

The innovators in this space deliver new services with increasing momentum by growing new tools out of the tools that came before them. On Monday, Google releases a new mapping capability. By Wednesday, some previously unheard of firm has built a mobile application to tie it to Facebook, and by Friday someone else has integrated that mobile application with Salesforce.com and is selling it on iTunes.

And again, these new innovative tools can be used by anyone who has an Internet connection. At the same time, technology is making it easier to compete, and these tools make it easier to compete from *anywhere*.

A small, even tiny business can access high-quality software tools for sales, invoicing, scheduling, reservations, communications, call centers and many other functions. Frequently, these tools are more effective than those used by businesses that invested millions of dollars writing their own systems. And sometimes they are free. Once again, David is well armed.

Internet-powered innovations are overturning an industrial-age standby: economies of scale. In the old model, scale provided resources that allowed organizations to offer better, more cost-effective solutions. But in the new world, competitors can adopt these cheaper and frequently more functional applications quickly.

The scale of the investment in established businesses makes it extremely difficult to muster the will to change. If they do finally begin to change, they incur significant costs to convert their data and their processes out of their established systems. While some businesses have had success shedding portions of their infrastructure, removing existing applications from inside an organization is very difficult. Applications that were designed to last a few years may run for decades. They become deeply entangled with other applications and in the processes of the business. Although they may be expensive to maintain and ill-designed for the tasks they perform, they are extremely hard to remove.

Meanwhile, small competitors have nothing to shed before adoption, nor do they have any sacred cows or pet projects to protect. Economies of scale yesterday can be a competitive disadvantage today, as existing systems weigh down the speed of modernization inside large corporations. David gains the advantage as Goliath becomes too sluggish to compete.

Technological Shift #2B: Utility Computing

The next new tool in David's belt is what people originally referred to when speaking of the ambiguous "Cloud." The power of basic computer capabilities—data processing, storage and communication—can now be accessed through sockets in our wall, like we access electricity, and many entrepreneurial businesses have begun to provide the key powers of the computer to anyone with an Internet connection. This "cloud" of capabilities (or this set of utilities, depending on your preferred metaphor) is once again a major change in the competitive landscape.

These innovations are not only impressive in themselves, but the innovation of Internet-powered services feeds mobile innovation by allowing the relatively puny power of mobile devices to tap into the vast data and processing power of the Internet. Cloud advances also increase the speed of investment in mobility by giving upstart businesses the tools to create new applications without having to invest in their own back-end infrastructure. These new businesses don't have to buy or even think about solutions to their infrastructure needs. It frees up their wallets, and more important, their minds to focus on other investments more critical to their business.

But the biggest implication for large organizations with significant technology investments is that the cloud nullifies many of the advantages of the large IT organization. No longer does a business need to own expensive, air-conditioned facilities with raised floors and intense security to have access to significant, secure computing power. All of it is available through the Internet and at a fraction of the cost.

With these advances, the small guy has just been given another new set of tools. This can't be good for large, hardly nimble corporations.

Technological Shift #3: Collaboration and Sharing

From its earliest days, the primary purpose of the Internet was collaboration: sharing data, files and email. The World Wide Web expanded that capability. The Web allowed users to find information that was difficult or impossible to find previously and allowed everyone to contribute to that information.

As with previous advances in PC and mobile computing, the innovation is predominantly on the consumer side—the Web is festooned with picture sharing, geo-tagging, social networking, trip planning, product-rating and advice-giving sites powered by the Internet that tap into basic human drives: connection, creativity, expression and altruism. And, all of it is virtually "free."

These advances in collaboration and sharing software introduce a new problem for businesses: customers have simultaneously become their company's best advertisers, fiercest competitors and worst critics. Already, information-intensive businesses (especially in entertainment and news) are facing competition from people who write, play music or compose videos just for the joy of it. In many cases, they are better at it, and their authenticity (which shines through because they are doing what they love) makes them more believable.

Look around your company. Public relations and marketing department heads are hanging pretty low as they watch disappointed customers create popular blogs or YouTube videos airing the dirty laundry of businesses. And, it feels as if there's nothing they can do to prevent it. As a result the marketing team tries to protect their jobs by blaming IT instead of proactively engaging the customer in constructive dialog.

In the meantime, leading-edge small businesses are using the power of Web-based tools and platforms (many of them free) to collaborate across distances, spur their own product creation and reduce costs. Start-ups can, without ever meeting in person, work with people from around the world and work together in unprecedented ways. They can hold online meetings in which everyone sees each other, views the same presentation, watches the same videos, edits the same files, and even writes on the same virtual whiteboard at the same time. These businesses can leverage the most talented people they can find, regardless of location and regardless of whether they are an employee, contractor, consultant, partner, customer, competitor, supplier or any other role.

This kind of Web-based collaboration renders irrelevant the artificial distinction between who is in a company and who is outside it. Good ideas can come from customers and suppliers, and those who would have seen themselves as competitors just a few years ago can join forces to create entirely new products and services literally overnight.

While older businesses choose to stay shackled to their office infrastructure, newer businesses have the ability to significantly reduce costs and, at the same time, allow talented resources to improve their lifestyles by working from home. As old-school business executives grumble about how employees who work from home will spend all day doing laundry, start-ups incorporate this new global workplace concept into their strategic plans. New technology has made expensive offices irrelevant as productive meetings can be held without a conference room. Even "water cooler" chat can be replaced with text messaging or one of the many new combined text, audio and video tools. The new David company is using collaboration as a competitive weapon, gaining cost, productivity and speed advantages while revolutionizing the way corporations evolve.

The new tools of technology discussed in this chapter, such as mobile devices and using the Internet as a platform, are advancing faster because they are being used in conjunction with each other. These collaboration tools empower developers and customers by providing them a means of sharing their ideas and problems *immediately*. In short, collaboration gets easier and fuels new forms of innovation. Each speeds up the pace of the other, and thus, speeds up the pace of creative destruction in existing industries and businesses that fail to adapt.

The 1990s rhetoric about the power of the Internet and the Web to change the business landscape may have been a bit premature, but it was on target. These technologies are remaking businesses; yet, the business models many companies put in place for addressing competition are outmoded and unproductive. For businesses to thrive in the new millennium, they must learn to think about technology systematically and strategically. They must harness its potential and reboot the way they currently work.

Now What?

Executives need a way to address all of these problems together—to help make sense of the changes and to actually *do* something about them. The next section introduces our system for thinking comprehensively about technology strategy—the kind of strategy that enables innovation and allows business executives to capitalize on the "speed frontier"—which is what David is using right now to leave Goliath standing in the dust.

Our strategy system has worked well for companies navigating the rapidly changing technology landscape. It begins with a **Model** used to organize ideas—both problems and solutions—with a group of people. Next, a scientific **Approach** is applied to provide a structured way of thinking based on the scientific method (although probably not the one you learned in school). Using this approach, a structured **Project** is constructed to organize the work of strategic thinking. Our system uncovers practical insights and drives strategic action. Parts of this system may appeal to you and parts may not. That's fine by us. Whether you use the exact system or not isn't the point.

Our sole mission is to inspire you to instill a similar methodology in your business, helping your company think strategically about how to use technology to compete. We call our system the **Strategy MAP**. It's not fancy like "the cloud," but quite honestly, we think a dose of practicality is overdue.

In an effort to stay grounded in practicality, let's take a guided tour of MAP.

SECTION 2

A NEW TWIST ON TECHNOLOGY STRATEGY

Chapter 3

The MAP Guided Tour
Lemons
Into Lemonade

here are so many opportunities out there—and so many threats. The technology landscape is rapidly changing and businesses need a way to navigate it. If you are feeling a little overwhelmed, know that you are in a better place than those who have their heads buried in the sand (or both heads in Goliath's case).

We've been there, that overwhelmed place where you might be now, have been before, or will be in the future. We've stared at the blank pieces of paper and slides on our computer screen. We've lost ourselves in the ideas jumbled all over the whiteboard. We've stared out the window. And while we still do all of that every once in a while, we've found some pretty effective ways of getting inspired and moving forward.

That's what we've packaged up for you here. It is the system we've been using the last few years to build executable, winning strategies. Our system uncovers practical insights and drives strategic action. It is a new twist on technology strategy, and we think you are going to like it. We call it the Strategy MAP.

If you have studied the strategic tools that make up the best business books, you'll recognize that this system is not a replacement for those models. It is meant to complement many of the other successful models people have applied in the past. However, throughout our careers using popular models, we found a major gap in the development of successful strategic thought-systems.

We were trained as computer scientists and spent our early careers building information technology systems. During those years, we became familiar with the struggles of actually delivering technology. We came to understand how difficult it is to build effective systems. It is also challenging to predict how those systems will be used "in the wild"—when they get into the hands of the people who need them. We observed how disjointed these huge systems integration investments were from

THE NEW CONSULTANT'S FIRST INTERVIEW

SO, OUR PROJECT IS GOING TO CATAPULT YOU INTO THE 21ST CENTURY. BY THE WAY, HOW LONG HAVE YOU WORKED HERE?

I STARTED HERE IN 1984. IT WAS MY SECOND JOB.

WOW! THAT WAS BEFORE I WAS BORN.

strategic business goals. As we moved through our careers, we became more and more appalled by the lack of integrated thought around strategic goals and their execution.

Many of the great books on business strategy virtually ignore technology as a component of business strategy. (Of course, many of them were written before technology *was* a component of business strategy.) Still, the academic world of the MBA teaches little about how to think about technology strategically. The C-level business world has few (if any) practical frameworks to help guide strategic thinking around technology. Needless to say, we think this is a gross oversight.

As our careers advanced and we focused more on the strategic application of technology, we began to synthesize ideas from our academic training, popular business books, and our practical experience. Once we established our own company, Thought Ensemble, we were able to freely apply our training and experience to build our own way of thinking about technology strategy to fill in the gaps.

Some good business strategy models do exist, such as Porter's Five Forces, the BCG Matrix, Balanced Scorecard, and SWOT to name a few; and we bring them into our strategy projects. They may be useful tools for thinking through a part of the problem, but these models don't help people and organizations with the process of strategic thinking. They don't cover the full spectrum needed to create visionary, executable strategies. We wanted something that would help us think through problems and solutions holistically. We also wanted an approach that would help us balance the need for analysis with the need to quickly identify the best solutions and move those into action. We wanted a process that would help us help organizations coordinate efforts in a way that was extremely effective but also incredibly fast.

The other gap we saw was the separation of business and technology strategies. Most models ignore the central issue of how to think strategically about business *as* technology transforms it. Because technology has become a driving force (some would say *the* driving force) in economic growth and industry restructuring, technological innovation is a dominant aspect of every company's strategic landscape, whether it is part of their strategic plans or not. Only by understanding the impact of rapidly evolving capabilities of technology, can we begin to understand the sweeping changes created by them. And only by thinking about them systematically, can we hope to clear up disjointed organizational behavior to shape the future before the competition does. The link between business and technology is at the heart of our system.

The MAP has the three major components required for strategic planning: a Model for structuring analysis, an Approach for thinking about the Model and a Project designed to ensure execution. The MAP provides a framework that enables businesses to assess key issues and challenges for the company. This system helps business leaders produce a strategic plan for the company's marketplace. It supports leaders in testing the strategic plan's feasibility and evaluating whether or not it is working.

We've discussed this system with leading business and technology thinkers and executives and debated it among our peers. We've studied companies around the world, and we've used this system repeatedly with our clients. We've refined it to focus on the most important issues facing any business wanting to win by leveraging technology. The system helps analyze and define the strategy itself, the technology that will realize it, and the methods and organization used to deliver it with a competitive edge. The insights in MAP came from the patterns we've seen across all of these disciplines. We have found it remarkably helpful in focusing attention and harnessing thought effectively.

As an introduction to the MAP system, let's consider one of the most important businesses ever conceived: the lemonade stand. This summertime children's activity has been a terrific training ground for many business professionals. It is the first time many children are exposed to the basic business concepts of cost, profit, marketing and operations. They learn they can drive revenues higher by locating the stand in areas where more cars drive by, with effective signage to encourage visitors. They learn how critical it is to keep revenues up by providing a high-quality product that keeps their customers coming back. They learn the trade-offs between a high-quality product and the cost of quality ingredients as they start to understand profit. The lemonade stand teaches many of the basics of running a business.

Occasionally (although less and less frequently) when we talk to business leaders, they doubt the importance of having a technology strategy. When we challenge them to come up with a business idea that does not appear to need a technology strategy, they sometimes cite the lemonade stand. Many people can't imagine how a lemonade stand could benefit from technology.

So, we put that notion to the test and rethought a childhood attempt at building a neighborhood lemonade stand, all the while asking, could technology provide a significant competitive advantage?

To introduce you to the technology Strategy MAP, we'll follow a young David as he seeks to build the most successful lemonade stand in his hometown, which will provide a guided tour of how our Strategy MAP works in relation to his business. Consider as you read how differently David is approaching a basic project. Instead of just going through the motions, David strives for competitive advantage as he reboots the summer lemonade stand.

David's Lemonade Stand

David was no ordinary twelve-year-old. He didn't just want to run an ordinary preteen lemonade stand. His older sister had already done that, and he saw no reason to simply follow in her footsteps.

He wanted to build the most successful lemonade stand known to man. He learned a little bit about business from his mom who ran a local electronics store, and grasped important concepts about technology from his dad who developed software for a company in town. He also learned a little bit about how to think systematically from his science teacher at school. And, yes, David was more than a little ambitious. He wanted to go back to school in September with a success story that would blow away his classmates and teachers.

When David first sat down at the kitchen table to think about the lemonade stand he planned to launch after school ended, his mind raced. He had hundreds of ideas. He could locate his stand at the major intersection in town, but that would require either his mom or dad to drive him and his supplies back and forth. That wasn't practical. He could put an ad in the local newspaper, but his parents only offered to invest fifty dollars to help get him started and advertising would consume the entire investment. Besides, he didn't know anyone who read the newspaper anymore except his grandparents.

But David also had some thoughts that involved technology. He considered using his Facebook account to attract customers to his lemonade stand. His parents let him set up an account two months ago, and he already had about thirty friends, and those friends had parents with cash. His mom ran a neighborhood email distribution list that discussed topics such as crime and neighborhood improvements, and David wondered if he could use that list. His dad volunteered with the local animal shelter just down the street and had a website that was frequently visited by many people in the neighborhood.

David also knew people were more likely to buy lemonade on hot and sunny days, so he considered using weather forecasting tools to choose which days he would be open for business. After all, it was summer, and he didn't want to work every day. He had opportunities to map out his competitors on Google Maps, create his own website, or even have his own blog. The possibilities were overwhelming.

After an hour of thinking about his business, David stared down at his notebook on the table—the page was still blank. He had too many ideas and wasn't making any progress. He needed a way to organize his thoughts. He needed a system that would help him win customers over the summer. So let's discuss how the Strategy MAP could help David get his lemonade stand up and running quickly.

The Strategy MAP is a system that solves the primary problems that David and all business leaders face when dealing with a myriad of strategic options:

1) **Focus:** David was lost in too many ideas, some of which were helpful, but others that would not boost his chances of success. He wanted to be comprehensive without getting lost in the minutia. The component of the Strategy MAP that addresses this need is the Model. It represents four major areas critical to the success of any technology strategy. The four areas of the Model are the strategy itself, the technology used to deliver that strategy, the delivery method for executing the strategy and lastly, the organization that supports that execution.

2) **Critical Thinking:** David didn't know how to tell good ideas from bad ones. He needed a way of thinking to help him determine which ideas were good and which ones did not really help him run the best lemonade stand ever. The component of the Strategy MAP that addresses this need is the Approach. It provides a scientific method for clearly defining a problem and working systematically to solve it by testing those ideas. The Approach is divided into three phases: problem definition, hypothesis creation, and tests and refinements.

3) **Execution**: David needed a method for moving himself and his ideas forward. He needed a way to move methodically from one stage to another so that he could quickly drive to conclusions without backtracking in his thinking. Otherwise he would continue to go in circles, never knowing where to start or finish. The component of the Strategy MAP that addresses

this need is the Project. It is a step-by-step, problem-solving structure designed to run a project focused on creating a technology strategy. The three steps of the Project are: assessment, vision and plan.

We will visit with David throughout the guided tour of MAP, and discuss how each component will affect his lemonade stand. Then, we will follow up with a detailed chapter on each component: Model (Chapter 4), Approach (Chapter 5) and Project (Chapter 6).

The Strategy MAP System

The Strategy MAP contains three major components, which added together constitute a single integrated system for thinking through technology strategy. They operate together. The Model is the basic structure for your ideas, both problems and solutions. Then the Approach helps move the ideas (within the Model) from problems and possible solutions to recommended actions. The Project helps with the steps to build the strategy, utilizing both the Approach and the Model. In theory, any one of these components could be used independently, and other components could be substituted. We've found that these components, used together as part of a system, help companies be most effective in their strategic planning efforts.

Strategy MAP System = Model + Approach + Project

Component 1: Model

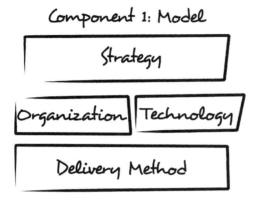

Component 2: Approach

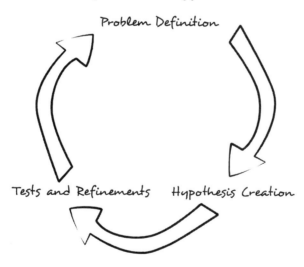

Component 3: Project

Now that we've introduced all of the components of MAP, let's take a step back and refocus on the end game. The goal of any business is to compete. Now that technology has become such a strategic imperative, corporations desperately need a way of efficiently organizing the process of thinking and testing new ideas. Most businesses don't understand that the game is being played a new way, with a whole new set of tools. With your help, your organization can grasp this.

We could start with any of the three components (Model, Approach or Project), but we chose to start with the Model for reasons other than it made for a nice acronym. We start with the Model component because it frames the analysis that is critical to the formulation of any strategy, even David's. It helps define the problems. It helps set scope. It gets you *thinking* before you jump into deep analysis or execution.

Which brings us back to David and all his great (or are they great?) ideas. He needs to remove some complexity and get focused if he is going to get the edge, allowing him to outmaneuver the competition.

Guided Tour of the Model

Again, we recommend starting with the Model component of the MAP system because it frames the analysis. It sets the level of strategic thinking that will be used in the other two components of the system. When presented with a new strategic challenge, we can easily lose focus. Many ideas present themselves, many current capabilities (and deficiencies) come to light, and many external threats and opportunities complicate the analysis. Like David, many people who are applying strategic thought get lost in myriad ideas and options. They need something to help structure their thinking. This is where the application of a Model can focus and shape the analysis and innovation.

The Model is intentionally simple. As discussed earlier, complicated mental models can trap people. This is particularly true when dealing with technology.

Most of the models floating around these days are so complex they require significant study, expensive training and practice to use them effectively. Their complexity ensures that only one or two people within the company can understand them sufficiently enough to work with them. We're not sure exactly what the reason is for the obsession with complexity, but we do know that technology strategy needs to be rebooted, and the complicated must be simplified in order to engage the right people in strategic thinking.

Simplicity is important because of the need for speed. Speed requires businesses to act with disciplined focus around a prioritized list of issues. A simple model will help establish the right focus and clearly communicate the strategy to others in the organization. This simplicity is one of the ways that smaller, more nimble companies are winning the innovation war. By virtue of their size, they naturally keep it simple, and thus, gain the advantage of speed.

Twelve-year-old David knows this, and like many global upstarts, that gives him the edge.

In the figure below, we indicate what each area of the Model is designed to accomplish.

The Model Component

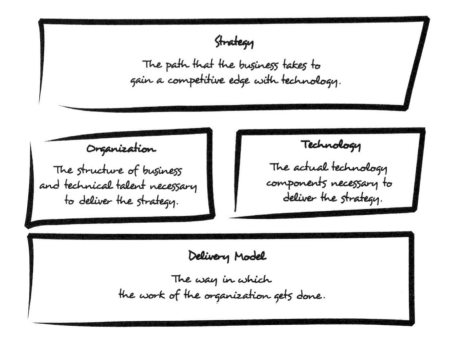

Strategy
The path that the business takes to gain a competitive edge with technology.

Organization
The structure of business and technical talent necessary to deliver the strategy.

Technology
The actual technology components necessary to deliver the strategy.

Delivery Model
The way in which the work of the organization gets done.

Now, let's look briefly at David's lemonade stand through the viewpoint of the Model. In the following example, David utilizes this component of the Strategy MAP for his business. A look at David's current opportunities and assets shows that he has a lot to work with.

Using the Model for the Assessment Step

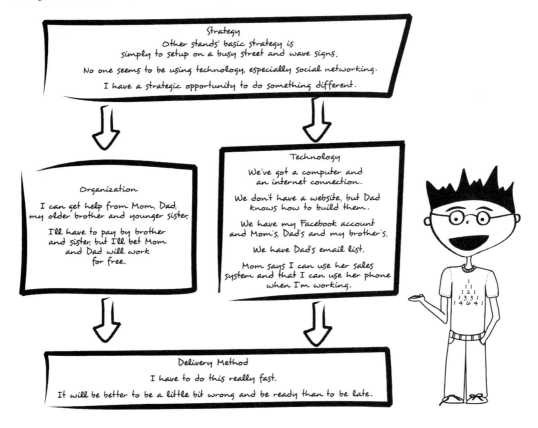

Strategy
Other stands' basic strategy is
simply to setup on a busy street and wave signs.
No one seems to be using technology, especially social networking.
I have a strategic opportunity to do something different.

Organization
I can get help from Mom, Dad,
my older brother and younger sister.

I'll have to pay by brother
and sister, but I'll bet Mom
and Dad will work
for free.

Technology
We've got a computer and
an internet connection.

We don't have a website, but Dad
knows how to build them.

We have my Facebook account
and Mom's, Dad's and my brother's.

We have Dad's email list.

Mom says I can use her sales
system and that I can use her phone
when I'm working.

Delivery Method
I have to do this really fast.
It will be better to be a little bit wrong and be ready than to be late.

David's lemonade stand is an intentionally simple example. Although we'll cover more complex examples in the next chapter, this step is designed to organize and effectively focus his ideas. It will help David make a list of his assets and ensure that he doesn't miss any of the key components necessary for a successful strategy.

Guided Tour of the Approach

The Approach component is based on a key principle of scientific thought: that the only practical way of coming up with an effective answer is to develop a variety of different options (hypotheses) and put them through critical examination until the best option emerges. While this may seem self-evident, when applied to business, it is a powerful way of thinking through a problem. A scientific approach encourages bold creativity, removes attachment to a particular idea, and focuses work on discovering what is wrong with any particular strategy rather than simply what is right about it.

How often have you seen a challenge identified, then a list of solutions created, with no real thought about the true implications of those possible solutions, much less an effective ruling-out process? Generally, whoever came up with the idea and has the most organizational power to bear tends to win the innovation battle. And that's exactly why Goliath companies are failing to innovate, as young upstarts usurp their customers across the globe. That way of operating in the face of incredible and rapid technological innovation has to change.

Now, in practice, it is best to break the Approach to strategic thinking into three distinct phases as listed below. The reason for this is simple: speed. Often, having a structured order to our thinking process can save time that would otherwise be spent endlessly going in circles. We'll break each of the phases of Approach down for you here during our guided tour and then dig into them more deeply in Chapter 5.

The Approach Component

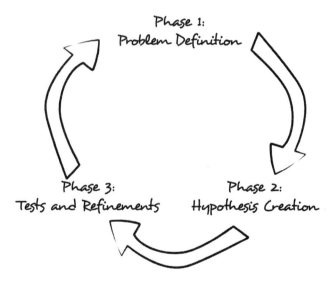

Phase 1:
Problem Definition

Phase 3:
Tests and Refinements

Phase 2:
Hypothesis Creation

Phase 1—Problem Definition: A clear definition of the problem is produced first. It surprises people that this is so difficult yet so critical to getting good results. As simple as it sounds, most businesses don't take the time to define the problem they are trying to solve and, consequently, end up wasting resources on symptoms rather than the root cause.

Phase 2—Hypothesis Creation: After the problem is defined, hypotheses are created that may address the problem. There may be several hypotheses to address a single problem. On the other hand, a single hypothesis may take care of multiple problems. Creating these hypotheses is often the hardest, most creative work of the project.

Phase 3—Tests and Refinements: In the final phase, several hypotheses are tested. Most often this is done by critical examination and discussion; however, analysis and data gathering can help

as well. Hypotheses will be changed and refined during this phase as criticisms and data help us to improve them. Some hypotheses will be jettisoned, and new ones may emerge, just as with any scientific journey. During this phase, final strategies are selected for implementation.

Now, let's turn our attention back to our hero, David, and his lemonade stand. David started with Phase 1, defining the problem. He looked at the current marketplace, some of the challenges of existing businesses, and ways he could launch his business to be unique and compete effectively. He thought that the biggest problem (or in this case, opportunity) was that most lemonade stands are independent, small businesses with no player owning the market space.

David used the second phase of the Approach to come up with a set of potential solutions (or hypotheses), in which he developed ideas on how to build a system. He wanted his system to: allow multiple kids to centrally order supplies and to communicate; implement his mom's sales tracking system; calculate the profits on each cup of lemonade; track all of his competitor's locations on Google maps; and send out an email to his Dad's mailing list, which would be inexpensive, quick and reach a lot of people. All of these hypotheses could be implemented in a way to link together multiple lemonade stands. In the third phase of the Approach, David tested his hypotheses by subjecting them to scrutiny via a discussion with his mom and dad. He had to question if it was a good idea to try to unite a variety of lemonade stands through technology, and whether he would be able to get help from his brother and sister if things took off. He questioned how important it was to know the location of his competition, and whether the finances of the business even made sense. And lastly, he determined if his dad would actually let him use his mailing list.

We'll explain how the Approach and Model components fit together in more detail in Chapter 5. For now, we will provide an overview of how the Project component is interconnected with these first two components in the Strategy MAP system.

Guided Tour of the Project

The Project component enables David to know where to start and what to do next. Many of us, especially when trying to coordinate with a variety of stakeholders, get lost in endless back and forth thinking, retracing our steps and needlessly extending the time until a solution is realized.

There are three steps to each Project. Step 1 is the *assessment*, step 2 is the *vision* and step 3 is the *plan*. Each of these steps will be discussed in more detail in Chapter 6; but for now, what you need to know is that these three easy steps are very helpful to individuals working on relatively small problems such as David's.

The primary purpose of the Project component is to organize a clear progression of steps for execution. However, it is even more potent when used with the large teams that are often necessary for technology strategy projects in large organizations. The Project component moves the team along, thereby preventing analysis-paralysis and ensuring major steps are not missed along the way. Consequently, it adds a sense of order to the way a strategy is delivered. This order increases a team's confidence in their steps and ensures the entire process can be effectively communicated up, down and across the organization.

The Project Component

- **Step 1—Assessment:** The assessment includes analyzing your business's external and internal world. In this step, you look at where you are, what you have to work with, what your customers (the real ones) need, and what your competitors are doing. The focus is on a clear, hard-nosed assessment of the current capabilities of the business, its technology, its delivery method and its organization. You also look out into the world to assess what is changing from a business and technology perspective and identify the opportunities and threats of those changes.

- **Step 2—Vision:** Vision involves the creation of the solution. In this step, you design where you want to be and what you'll need to get there. The hardest creative work of the project is completed here: designing a solution that will fill the strategic needs of the organization. The focus is on bold creativity and transformational design of new solutions. You create a new vision for using technology strategically.

- **Step 3—Plan:** The plan outlines the actions to be taken to deliver the strategic vision. You build a plan (or set of plans) to transform the existing technology, delivery method, and organization into the new vision. The focus is on setting practical steps and measurable criteria for the realization of the strategy. You build a roadmap for the various projects it will take to get to the vision you created. You estimate costs, timelines, and dependencies for each project in your overall plan.

In this system, David began his Project by doing a quick assessment. As described earlier, David used the Model to conduct that assessment. During the assessment, David looked critically at all of his assets: his current strategy (since he was starting from scratch and didn't have an existing strategy), the technology he could leverage, the delivery method he was going to use and the organization that could deliver it. He looked at both the internal and external environment, and because he was just starting out, he naturally had more of an external focus.

The Project component guided David through an orderly progression of strategic thinking. It helped him focus on conducting an assessment first, not on leaping ahead to strategy development or working through a tactical execution plan.

Having completed his assessment, David then had a realistic view of what he had to work with and could move on to the second step: vision. Once again, David used the Model to structure his vision. It looked something like this.

Using the Model for the Vision Step

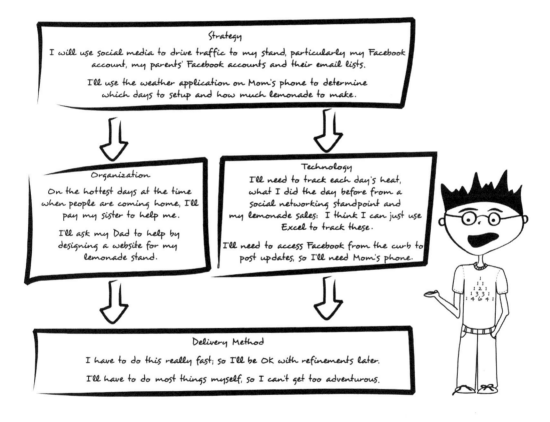

Strategy

I will use social media to drive traffic to my stand, particularly my Facebook account, my parents' Facebook accounts and their email lists.

I'll use the weather application on Mom's phone to determine which days to setup and how much lemonade to make.

Organization

On the hottest days at the time when people are coming home, I'll pay my sister to help me.

I'll ask my Dad to help by designing a website for my lemonade stand.

Technology

I'll need to track each day's heat, what I did the day before from a social networking standpoint and my lemonade sales. I think I can just use Excel to track these.

I'll need to access Facebook from the curb to post updates, so I'll need Mom's phone.

Delivery Method

I have to do this really fast; so I'll be OK with refinements later.

I'll have to do most things myself, so I can't get too adventurous.

David's strategy was substantially different from his competitors, and while the strategy may have seemed simple, that summer he was very likely to have significantly more success than his competitors. *A simple strategy is frequently a winning strategy.* David then took his vision and created a *plan* (the third step of the Project component) to implement his vision. He had a couple of other projects to complete before he could fully implement his strategy, such as designing the website, building out his Facebook account, gathering all his supplies, and setting up his first week's calendar.

Over the next three chapters, we will explore these ideas in detail and evaluate how the Strategy MAP can help Goliath companies compete against the nimble, quick, and well-tooled start-ups that are popping up around the globe.

CHAPTER 4

MODEL

ORGANIZING THOUGHT

Stanford physicist George E. Box once wrote, "All models are wrong, but some models are useful." He was, of course, writing about scientific models, but the same can be said of the various business models we have all used over the years. There are dozens (probably hundreds) of different mental models used in businesses: financial models, process models, organization models, etc. And, of course, there are many models that show how technology works with the rest of a business.

Models like these help us organize our thoughts and structure our solutions. Without some kind of mental model, thinking tends to become too unstructured, loose, and vague. And yet, most models that involve technology are spectacularly complex. Perhaps it's because technologists know how complex the technological world is and they want to make certain they address all of the complexity.

The model we review in this chapter is designed to answer a simple question, "If I were in charge of the strategic use of technology in my business, what would I need to think about?" We've divided the model into four main areas, the strategy, the technology, the delivery method, and the organization. Like Box, we hope that this is a *useful* way of categorizing the problems and solutions of technology strategy.

We begin with the first area of the Model: strategy. We always start with strategy, because everything hinges on it. As we explain how the Model functions, we provide examples of real corporate challenges we've encountered, and share ideas about how to resolve those challenges. The chapter concludes with more practical discussion for application of the Model to address your company's challenges.

Model Area 1—Strategy

"Strategy" is one of those words that excites some people, makes others' hair prickle, and causes others to roll their eyes in annoyance. People use the word in many ways: to describe their clever approach to a conversation with their boss or spouse, to describe how an entire company will achieve its objectives or to describe plans for war with another country.

When dealing with information technology, the word "strategy" gets even more gummed up. As consultants, when we tell people that we do "technology strategy," there are usually a variety of well-meaning follow-up questions:

"Ah, like data center consolidation?"

"So you design software?"

"Do you do process re-engineering?"

While these are good questions, they aren't quite right. Although they are good ideas to consider in the overall technology strategy, the bigger picture is broader. IT executives face similar challenges. When they attempt to define technology strategy, they often hear views on the stated and unstated needs of their business; and they often end up with a strategy that encapsulates everything their organization could do, bundled into one long, run-on sentence.

Strategy

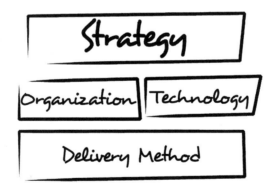

A Few Questions to Ask About Strategy

- What has our technology strategy been to date—explicit or implicit?
- What business goals do we want to achieve?
- How does technology enable or drive those goals?

So what is strategy? Specifically, what is technology strategy?

We had some fun looking up definitions of "strategy" and "technology strategy." It isn't worth the paper to repeat any of them. If you're curious, use your favorite search engine to see what you find.

For now, we will define strategy as choosing a direction, choosing what you want to be and what you are going to do to get there. Perhaps more important, it is choosing what you are not going to be and what you are not going to do.

Technology strategy has become a critical component of an overall business strategy (some would say *the* critical component). For many companies, like it or not, technology isn't even a subset: technology is either the critical enabler of its business strategy, or technology is the business itself.

The bottom line is that in order to compete, companies have to capitalize on technology, and they have to do it with speed. They must innovate more quickly to stay (or get) ahead of their competition.

As we move forward in our discussion, rather than using the simplistic lemonade stand, let's explore the real world challenges of a typical company and talk through some possible technology strategy solutions. To illustrate the power of the Model, we should first identify what isn't working in technology strategy, in order to focus on how to reboot it.

Strategy Challenge 1: IT Narcissism: Why "Operating Like a Business" Focuses on the Wrong Thing—Internal "Customers"

One of the most common issues is "IT narcissism." We realize this might be inflammatory, but hear us out. What surfaces as the technology strategy within many businesses is really an internal organizational plan for an IT department. The focus is around running the IT organization instead of producing technology that helps the business compete. This just isn't sufficient in a world in which technology is a strategic weapon.

Instead of thinking about how to use technology to change the way the business competes, the IT organization focuses on improving its services to internal customers, customers they often call "the business," as if the IT people themselves are not part of "the business." They are often solely concerned about risk management and cost containment. As mentioned in the first chapter, this is generally the wrong focus. It is too internally driven and certainly not how the snappy little David company is thinking.

You may have seen this process before. Someone hands the IT team a list of carefully worded "business objectives," which have been written in such a way as not to offend anyone. Then the IT guys take those objectives, try to guess what they meant before they were wordsmithed by committee, and come up with their own "aligned" objectives. It can make for a beautiful-looking PowerPoint presentation, but it doesn't say much in the way of strategy.

This inward focus has profound consequences. Most important, the expertise of the leaders who understand technology best is redirected to budgets, risk management, and "responsiveness" to internal customers rather than on envisioning new ways to harness the transformative power of technology to grow the business.

Admittedly, a few positive results have emerged from this inward way of thinking, primarily in moving IT organizations to behave with discipline and business savvy. However, viewing "the business" as a customer encourages CIOs and other IT leadership to think like an external service provider instead of as a member of a business team. This service provider mentality has effectively rendered IT replaceable. Replacing an internal IT organization with a set of external service providers might not ruin a business, but missing the opportunity to use technology to forward the strategic aims of the business likely will. Isn't it a bit ironic that this inward focus is likely to result in the organization getting outsourced?

This is not how David thinks about technology strategy. David will learn about a technological advancement and quickly organize a team to exploit it, stealing customers and their dollars. Meanwhile, Goliath sleeps in his cave, caring for his internal "customers."

The first step to reversing this navel gazing is to accept the problem. This doesn't mean that the work done around improving service to internal customers is wrong, it just means it cannot be the sole priority going forward. Everyone involved in defining the go-forward strategy must understand and embrace the need to focus externally.

In addition, getting to the right strategy requires getting the right business *and* technology people together. This is not a job for an isolated group of tech folks, no matter how knowledgeable and brilliant they are. Organizations have tried this divided approach to tech strategy for years—with less than stunning results.

The complexities of understanding a marketplace, understanding customer needs, understanding the technology entering that market, and knowing what to do about it, all require a multidisciplinary team of experts from various parts of the business.

Of course, technology people will be heavily involved and may be leading the effort, but they should not try to go it alone. Going it alone increases the risk of missing opportunities, decreases the likelihood of game-changing solutions, and increases the likelihood that nothing at all will occur because the whole organization has not bought into the strategy.

Strategy Challenge 2: Multiple Personality Disorder: Why Trying To Be Everything Results in Nothing

We recently came across a strategic plan from a top strategy firm. It began with an assessment that was both comprehensive and insightful. The strategy that followed presented several potential paths the company could take to grow its business. Again, it was pretty insightful. And then, someone wussed out. They never presented a choice between the paths the business could take. They never forced a decision. They tried to be all things to all people; and so, not surprisingly, they did nothing. It could have been the strategy firm, could have been the CEO, we do not know. We were just reading the strategic plan off the shelf. Of course, the result of this was our client was floundering, trying to focus on everything without clear priorities.

When building technology strategies, it is tempting to roll together every idea or request that anyone has ever had into one long, all-encompassing run-on sentence, like, "We will deliver innovative, high-quality solutions and services to the market faster and at continually lower costs by focusing on growing people and knowing our customers and by understanding our market and technology better than anyone through research and insightful thinking."

You may be thinking that this is an exaggeration, but we have seen similar strategy "vision" statements. By covering everything, strategies like this say nothing. Executives shrug their shoulders because it all sounds good, but they secretly fear it is meaningless. Jaded employees (many of whom have seen dozens of such statements) roll their eyes because they know the strategy sets lofty, yet vague, expectations that cannot be achieved.

These kinds of strategies are usually the result of excellent intentions. A team working on the technology strategy sets out to interview key business executives, each of whom details a laundry list of specific needs (frequently needs that are very tactical). The team working on the strategy quickly comes to realize that the executives want a lot of different things. No one wants to make hard choices. There is no prioritization: everything must be better, faster, and cheaper.

Sometimes this disorder is implicit rather than explicit. No one in the organization knows what the real strategy is; they just hear about the competition and the changing market and desperately try to react to it. They are overwhelmed with priorities, never knowing what's most important to work on or what should drive their decision-making. We humorously describe this as the two-headed Goliath who has gained multiple personalities to go with each head. A schizophrenic, two-headed Goliath is not a nimble or effective competitor.

Whether explicit or implicit, the result of this multiple personality disorder is that few in the organization, if any, are trying to move in the same direction. Those lower down in the organization unintentionally subvert decisions because they don't understand the context in which they are made. As with the previous strategy challenge, the first step is to accept the problem. Then work together with all the stakeholders to choose a strategic path that actually sets a direction.

Strategy Challenge 3: Annual Budget Subservience—Why the Budget Is Necessary but Not Sufficient

One process in every company seems to cause more damage than any other: annual budgeting. This process is a sort of grotesque dance where everyone hates their dancing partner, hates the music, and can't wait for it to be over. Horrible behavior erupts during the annual budget reviews: politicking, backstabbing, squirreling away dollars,

OUR ANALYSIS SHOWS WE CAN GET OVER 3000 NEW CUSTOMERS AND BRING IN $2,000,000 OF NEW REVENUE JUST BY COMPLETING THE FIRST PHASE OF THIS PROJECT.

MORE IMPORTANTLY, OUR COMPETITORS WON'T BE ABLE TO COPY OUR DESIGN.

CERTIFICATION TO BE A CEO

AND, WE'VE GOT ALMOST EVERYTHING ALREADY, SO IT WILL ONLY COST US A COUPLE THOUSAND DOLLARS.

CERTIFICATION TO BE A CEO

THAT'S NICE, BUT IT ISN'T IN THE BUDGET, SO LET'S SAVE IT FOR NEXT YEAR'S PRIORITIZATION PROCESS.

CERTIFICATION TO BE A CEO

nasty competition, and all sorts of spreadsheet gimmickry. But it is the worst around technology spending.

Every business needs a budget. Most departments need one, too. Technology investments are especially important because they have become such a significant portion of yearly capital expenditures and ongoing expenses. But making technology investment decisions based on simplistic budgetary planning, rather than a strategic analysis of how technology can be used to gain a competitive advantage in the marketplace, is catastrophic. This isn't how David thinks. A David company doesn't develop technology strategy within the constraints of an annual budgeting cycle.

The annual budgeting timeframe may seem like a logical time for some strategic thinking, since the various parts of the business are working through plans for next year. While it is possible that strategic thinking could come out of this process, the odds are against it. Annual budgeting is generally focused entirely on prioritizing projects that have already been proposed—it is mainly an exercise in prioritization and politicking, not deep thinking. Many organizations have tried to build up the annual planning and budgeting process to include some sort of business systems planning, but because of competing priorities, few of these make it into the annual plan.

Budgets are about cost containment and risk reduction, not about market analysis and creative thinking. The standard top-down, numbers-focused process puts people right in the middle of the constraints that they should be trying to avoid. The conversation is over before it starts. Real strategic thinking must take place outside the annual budget cycle if the organization is going to do anything truly innovative.

So what to do? What if your company's budget was driven first by strategic priorities, such as product innovation or technology innovation? Or, what if your company started by separating strategic thinking from the annual budget process? Annual planning, budgeting, and investment approval processes could be stripped to their bare minimum. These activities are important but must be simplified to keep the organization on track toward its goals.

Your leadership team should spend more time talking about real technology strategy than they do about hitting the numbers. Don't let the budget consume you. It will, if you let it.

Now that we've talked through some of the major challenges and solutions with technology strategies, you are probably already bubbling up several hypotheses for what the strategy in your organization might be. As we move into the technology area, consider how your current set of technology is supporting that strategy.

Model Area 2—Technology

The technology in established companies generally is a hodgepodge of new and old, half-implemented systems, many of which were the mistakes and successes of predecessors, such as ancient hardware and out-of-date and unsupported software. Often, companies believe they have only one guru who understands their architecture. In reality, no one understands the architecture completely. The technology landscape in most businesses looks like it was never designed or architected at all.

The existing technology can be both a benefit and a drawback for businesses: the complexity and disorganization can slow down innovation and increase maintenance costs, but the vast resources of data and processing power can also be powerful assets. The challenges we'll talk through here are common in companies that have been around for a few years. Newer companies have the arguably easier challenge of starting from ground zero.

Technology

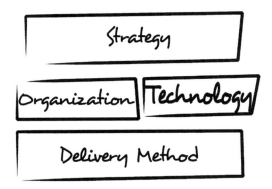

A Few Questions to Ask About Technology

- How are our applications helping us to compete in the market today?
- Where are the redundancies? Gaps?
- Are the integrations between the systems helping our employees and customers access the data they need efficiently?
- How can we better leverage the data we have as a competitive advantage?
- How is the technical health of our application portfolio?
- Is our infrastructure supporting current and future needs?

Technology Challenge 1: Complexity—Goliath's Biggest Handicap

In any sizable company that is more than a few years old, the complexity of the technology infrastructure is daunting. Even companies with strong architectural standards find that technology changes so quickly that each of their major systems is likely to be built on a different underlying technology. Most companies have a diverse group of business systems, built on a diverse set of software technologies, running on a diverse platform of hardware, tied together by a diverse group of integration technologies. "Complex" sometimes seems too wimpy a word to describe the bewildering intricacy of the existing technology infrastructure.

Often the complexity simply arises from the rocket-fast evolution of technology, but business practices drive even more complexity. The most common is the rogue system phenomenon. When business units go off on their own (frequently because of the organizational challenges mentioned previously) to buy or build solutions, they create new systems outside the normal rigors of the business. These rogue systems perform some of the most critical functions of the business, but are also frequently the least secure, most buggy, and most likely to fail. While often not captured in the IT spend, the expense to maintain them can be significant. Over time, the cumulative effect can be substantial and extremely hard to fix.

In addition to rogues, we often find a slew of partially implemented systems. At the outset of their development, plans no doubt existed to complete each one; but budget constraints, project delivery problems, or other issues left behind a hodgepodge of underperforming systems. These systems slow down their human users, present the wrong data to internal employees and customers, and cause bad decision-making across the organization. In addition, incomplete systems have a high likelihood of placing higher demands on surrounding systems because they are not well-structured.

Many other causes of unnecessary complexity in technology exist in our businesses: redundant systems built for political reasons, projects launched with no real justification, products built following development fads, systems that were not retired because of one or two strong-willed users, etc. Complexity has an enormous impact on speed and cost, but is rarely addressed as a problem in its own right.

Let's tell a dirty little secret here. In a weird way, most IT organizations are proud of this complexity. It's as if they believe that this complexity must mean that their architecture is sophisticated and, therefore, a competitive advantage.

Wrong. Simplifying technology architecture is the *only* way to move a company along faster. Remember, speed is the new frontier. You already know the speed advantages David has over Goliath with his new tools. So, if you want to compete with speed, there's no choice but to shift your technology from complexity toward simplicity.

Yet, instead of trying to simplify their technology infrastructure, organizations allocate the dominant portion of their information technology spending to maintenance and to new projects that often add to the complexity. Few companies invest in reducing the complexity of their existing systems. When you look at the world from the competitive landscape of speed and realize that complexity slows you down, it just seems downright crazy.

Many Goliath companies need to prune existing systems. Technology tends to get a bit weedy over time: systems that have sprouted up in the wrong place need to be removed, cut back, and pruned. Some of these systems can be simply turned off. Some of them will have to have their functionality merged into other applications. In many businesses, systems duplicate functionality that runs elsewhere two or three times. These systems must be consolidated or retired.

People may fight it. They like the peculiarities of their specific systems and will claim their business will come to a halt or revenue will be lost without it; but in order to simplify the overall architecture, some of these systems must be removed.

Technology Challenge 2: Safety—Goliath's Biggest Blind Spot

At first glance, safety may not seem like a problem in technology—it might even be viewed as a positive trait. But overly safe investments over decades have produced technology architectures that do nothing to differentiate businesses from their competitors.

Much of the investment in technology has been sucked up by business management systems (e.g., ERP systems, such as SAP and Oracle, or commoditized billing or sales systems). These comfortable systems may improve operational efficiency and management decision-making, but they offer little advantage over the norm in the industry. Basically, these large "investments" in technology have more to do with organizing internally focused processes than they do with providing direct value to customers.

In almost any industry, there are sets of "safe" systems that look very much the same across companies. These commoditized systems are the reason some pundits say IT is dead. Not only is there no competitive advantage to these safe systems, decades of investment in these systems has constrained creativity in other areas. There are entire industries made up of businesses that are essentially technology clones of each other. David looks at industries full of cloned Goliaths and sees weaknesses he can exploit. The search for safety and risk aversion has left many established businesses ready to be attacked by new entrants.

The SaaS (Software as a Service) trend that we discussed in Chapter 2 offers a new alternative for managing the commodity (cloned) portions of our businesses. Not all of IT is a commodity, but much of it is. Not all business practices are standard across companies, but many are. In general, businesses should not be building things from scratch that can be bought off the shelf or rented from the information grid. Businesses should focus instead on things that will differentiate them from the competition. Read that sentence again! The reason to use SaaS is to redirect those basic investments into innovation through technology that can set you apart from your competition, not just to cut costs.

At first glance, this recommendation may seem obvious, but it runs counter to the way technology investment occurs in most businesses. Most investment in businesses still goes into standard business management systems: billing, revenue management, call centers, online shopping carts, etc. In other words, investment goes into those systems that make businesses into clones of each other. Very little goes into new investments or into improving systems that are already a differentiator.

Okay, let's move to the third area of the Model and focus on how businesses operate around technology. Again, think back to your hypotheses on what your strategy should be and consider the kinds of technology you need to deliver on that strategy. You likely have a big gap between what you have currently and where you want to be. The right delivery method will help you get there.

Model Area 3—Delivery Method

The *delivery method* is the way people come together to get things done. In the lingo of the Strategy MAP, this is the combination of processes, methodologies, working methods, meeting management, annual cycles and more, that are the actual work that gets done in an organization to deliver technology. In the end, it is the way a company goes about delivering on a strategy that will determine whether that strategy will be successful. Fumbling during delivery will render even the best strategy useless.

The delivery method for a technology strategy includes the processes a team follows as well as its daily habits, such as its meeting schedule, its communication mechanisms, and the tools it uses.

Remember, the Model component of MAP is about organizing thought. In this case, the thought is about how technology solutions could or should be delivered.

Delivery Method

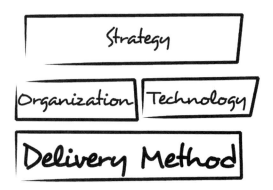

A Few Questions to Ask About Delivery Method

- What are the processes we use to support delivery of our technology?
- Where are the root causes of our issues?
- Where can we streamline these processes?
- What have we accepted as a way of working that has become inefficient or ineffective over time?

Delivery Challenge 1: Myopic Solutions—The #1 Reason Process Improvement Fails

Many businesses have very good intentions around process improvement. They identify a weak area and attack it. Maybe it is project management, new employee provisioning, trouble tickets, or annual planning. They send in a team to diagnose this specific problem and recommend a solution. In most cases, the team recommends good solutions, and they optimize the individual process. However, unintended consequences often cause the rest of the system to become less efficient.

Let's look at a simple example. Take a group tasked with improving their requirements-gathering process. They look at the problem and determine that they don't have good written documentation, so they recommend a formal sign-off of requirements before development can begin. This change yields better requirements, but it slows down the overall development process. The problem may have been real, but the resolution of the problem was not seen in the context of the overall, end-to-end system, and the results may be lowered productivity, missed opportunities, and retarded innovation.

End-to-end does not mean where things start and end in IT. It means looking at processes from suppliers all the way through to customers for new approaches to getting things done. It involves identifying and revamping the broader business processes that may be considered constraints. Piecemeal changes usually don't have a significant effect.

We see organizations with strategic priorities for delivering the most innovative solutions to their customers, but their delivery methods emphasize cost containment and long deliberation. The business executives can't understand why delivery is taking so long, and the technology executives can't understand why the business people don't appreciate how much money they are saving.

Delivery methods are best improved by picking an area that needs improvement and then expanding the scope just wide enough to get to the root causes and dependencies. Make sure the view is end-to-end and holistic enough (meaning looking at the organization and technology supporting it) to ensure the overall outcome is improved.

Once the new process is envisioned, the fun part begins. We've said this before, but it bears repeating. Simplify, simplify, simplify. Your goal is not to create a monster, interrelated, step–by-step, 100-page manual; your goal is to boil the process down to the minimal number of steps possible to meet your end strategic objective. If you can get it on one page, then all the better. You'll know when you are done; the group will breathe easier and wonder why it was so hard in the first place. And then you can take a fresh look at the organization and technology surrounding and supporting the process and make simplifications there as well.

Delivery Challenge 2: Process "Sacred Cows"—How Process Got a Black Eye

Whether it is the annual financial planning cycle that injects rigidity into strategic thinking, procurement processes that weed out excellent vendors, HR processes that prevent the hiring and firing of

employees, or technology governance processes that force a one-size-fits-all approach onto every project, processes can destroy value.

People who have spent any time in modern businesses know that sometimes the hardest thing to do is to get things done that don't fit into the standard processes of the organization. Yet, usually the most important work going on in any business is *outside* the standard processes of the business.

In many organizations, overly standardized processes have become the justification for delays and missed deadlines, and the reason bad decisions are made.

Processes have become the master. People serve the process rather than the process serving the people. Often, people lose sight of the outcome they want to achieve while waiting for the next step in the process. Overly rigorous and complex business processes can smother organizations. They can also cost a lot of money to maintain and can severely limit innovation.

For example, we've seen businesses try to speed up the time it takes to build new technology solutions for customers. They work endlessly on trying to improve the requirements-gathering part of the development methodology in IT, but they don't realize that the biggest delay is the annual budget or the project-approval cycles.

To make matters worse, vendors peddle a variety of *delivery methods* to businesses, promising to change their world. While many of them can add value, models like ITIL, CMM, COBIT, and others are not the be-all and end-all of process optimization. These models can be helpful, but they share a common limitation: they are focused on the commonalities, not the differentiators. They might make you more standardized, but they won't make you different, creative, or innovative.

Sometimes, the process frameworks IT has committed to must be challenged. Perhaps a decision was made to follow ITIL, which has worked well in operational process areas. But the ITIL prescription for development processes may not work as well for the same company.

To improve the way technology is delivered, businesses have to remove the constraints that lock them in. Higher-level business processes are often seen as sacred cows that can't be touched and have to be worked around. But if a business really wants to deliver technology quickly and efficiently, it must be willing to look at, and change, these broader processes.

So have a little fun and refuse to accept the constraints. That's what David is doing!

Delivery Challenge 3: Playing Whack-a-mole

Have you ever watched kids (or adults for that matter) play the game Whack-a-mole? They take a bat covered in foam padding and whack little mechanical moles as they pop up from holes on the game console. Whack more moles, get more points. That is how many people in business feel about their lives.

Clear out the email you received since last night when you went to bed: Whack-a-mole!

Attend the third meeting for the day (before lunch): Whack-a-mole! Whack-a-mole! Whack-a-mole!

An email comes in needing immediate response. Whack-a-mole!

Respond to a customer complaint: Whack a-mole!

Respond to the sixteen calendar invites you received since lunch. Whack-a-mole! Whack-a-mole! Whack-a- mole! You get the idea.

The grown-up version of this game isn't nearly as much fun as the kid's version. We know people who literally have thirty to forty meetings and well over 500 emails per week. In the average business day, there is little time for a few minutes of thought, much less the time it takes to analyze a problem thoughtfully. Goliath organizations, in particular, require their executives to focus so much on management and politicking that these people rarely have time to consider anything strategic. Is it any wonder that it is hard to get people to focus on finding the root causes of problems when they don't feel like they can go to the bathroom without taking their phones with them to check email?

To improve the overall delivery of an organization, people (at least *some* people) in the organization must be given enough slack in their calendar to spend time on the things that really matter, not just the things that are urgent.

Moving on to the final area of the Model, we now focus on the organizations that support the strategy, technology, and delivery method of the business. We saved *organization* for last because it is most dependent on choices in the other areas.

Model Area 4—Organization

Internal IT organizations and their people have been the source of complaints and the butt of jokes for years. Despite late hours and hard work, despite being on call for crashing computers in the middle of the night, and despite the fact that they are absolutely critical to the organization—IT is frequently one of the least-respected groups in the business. In the past, it was assumed that IT people couldn't blend well with the "normal" business folks, so they were deliberately cocooned away from the rest of the company. Is it a coincidence that this was around the time Goliath was growing his second head? That's probably a rhetorical question by now. This isolation further increased the feeling of distance among colleagues and made it hard to come together as a team for strategic thinking and action.

Although this division is common, the manner in which companies organize the people who plan, build, and run technology is constantly changing; and most companies have tried many different models through the years. Large companies engage hundreds, if not thousands, of people to manage the technologies they use to run their businesses. These people may work directly for the company or, increasingly, may be employed by outsourcers, consultancies, or other service providers. The diversity of "IT groups" in businesses has grown enormously, as the complexity of managing a variety of types of permanent and temporary employees has expanded. Even small organizations, which only have a person or two acting as technical problem-solvers, frequently employ external people or organizations to take on major projects.

The variations in organizational structure are endless, but the challenges we see across companies are pervasive.

Organization

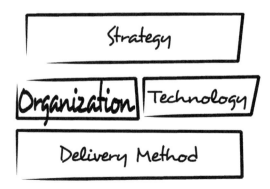

A Few Questions to Ask About Organization

- How do we describe our organization's culture?
- What capabilities do we need as an organization? What do we have?
- Are incentives aligned with the overall strategy?
- Are roles and responsibilities clear and optimized?
- Are layers of reporting structure and team sizes optimized?
- Are we using external vendors optimally to support our strategic goals?

Organization Challenge 1: Culture Clash—The Root of All Problems or the Source of All Solutions?

In most companies, the division between the people who work in IT and the rest of the company is immediately apparent. Whether talking to IT people or people who work in marketing, operations, finance, HR, or any other department of the organization, we get an earful of stories at every cocktail party—stories that are likely percolating through the organization and preventing strategic change. Some of these will probably sound familiar.

Stories from the IT department:

"We work crazy hours to complete projects against unrealistic expectations, and then when we deliver it, they don't even use it."

"They overpromise to the customer and then expect us to deliver. It always makes us look bad in the end."

"They say that they want us to be innovative, but they keep cutting our budgets. We're just glorified order takers. We're second-class citizens."

Stories from other (non-IT) departments:

"They say they want to be our Trusted Advisor, but all they do is drown me in processes and documentation. They make everything difficult."

"They are so expensive and slow that we are forced to go outside to get anything done."

"All I hear is 'no.' I wish they would present to me some options on how I could get what I need."

Clearly, something has gone awry. It appears IT organizations cannot work well with the other areas of their businesses to deliver anything, much less strategy. It appears these business people are ungrate-

ful, unreasonable, and abusive. Neither side seems willing to admit the obvious: they are in this together, and the only way to successfully take advantage of technology change is to change the way IT is organized. Meanwhile, the gap is only widening.

This is not an easy problem to solve because the damage is deep not only within businesses, but throughout the corporate world. People have come to expect that you should dislike your IT group. Tech people expect that their peers across their businesses just don't get it. And since these issues started a couple decades ago, many workers have never known anything different.

Part of the problem is that people often don't care about IT unless something goes wrong with it. Whether it's a network outage, a delayed project or even a new project that threatens to change the way people are comfortable doing things—all news is bad. About the best thing that can happen is an IT person coming to save the day when something is already broken. So best-case scenario, one person may be elevated to hero status amidst the sea of dissatisfaction.

IT people often don't help the situation. They communicate poorly about issues. They force business people to implement the wrong systems because they like the technology. They are sticklers about their policies and standards. It's all done with good intentions, but ineffective nonetheless.

You may be nodding your head right now, yet at the same time wondering what in the world to do about it. Something has to change.

When organizations go through a strategic change, the traditional approach has generally been to begin with setting up the organizational structures, then moving on to designing the capabilities, processes, or functions that support it, and finally (if they still have any energy) to thinking through the culture and values of the organization.

We recommend the reverse.

Start with culture and values. Understand where the culture is today, what the values are and what stories are being told. Lay out a vision for a new culture that is more likely to deliver in the way most appropriate for the company. This culture will be the foundation for discussions on designing the organization and its key capabilities.

A team aligned on values can move more swiftly than those that waste time and emotional energy on value conflicts, backbiting, internal sabotage, gossip, and bickering. Structure is less important when a team is focused on common values. And that team needs to include everyone who uses technology, not just the IT organization.

Then comes the really hard part. Live the values, with the top of the organization setting an example for everyone. Recognize and reward individuals who demonstrate these values. Hire people who exemplify these values. Fire those who don't.

If you can get this right, the rest will be much easier to implement. So, if you can only do one thing well, then do this: build an organization that has shared values, regardless of its structure or processes.

Organization Challenge 2: Capability Crisis—Why Building Talent in IT is a Whole Different Ballgame with a Different Set of Rules

Maintaining technology skills is notoriously difficult. The pace of technology change in the last few years has made staying abreast of technology trends even more challenging. To maintain current skills, technology professionals require frequent study. In most organizations, they are not afforded the time or budget to complete this kind of study. During financial crises, training budgets are some of the first to be cut, but technology innovation itself doesn't halt.

The capability gap goes beyond eroding technical know-how. Technology skills are important, yes, but it is the surrounding capabilities that enable an IT organization to affect change. Tech people, bless our hearts, don't usually pop out of computer science programs with strong communication and leadership capabilities. Although technology expertise may be the most important quality for a junior employee, by the time that employee is in an executive role, these skills are far overshadowed by the need for other capabilities. Most IT organizations offer little training or coaching of critical management and leadership skills.

When the individuals in a business fall behind, so does the business as a whole. The business begins to fall back on a few people who manage to keep up. They somehow are able to stay current, and above all, they know how to get things done. These heroes are pulled from project to project, placed on the most important initiatives to the organization and generally deployed to make up for the limitations of the rest of the organization. For a while, these heroes receive special treatment. They get their way and they get things done, but because they are continuously pulled from crisis to crisis, they find less and less time for study and for improving their skill-sets. Today's hero slowly degrades into tomorrow's out-of-date, burned-out employee.

Many well-meaning HR departments have tried to help with these challenges, to no avail. In no other area of the business does the know-how required to do a job change as fast as it does in technology. And in few other areas are the capabilities necessary to succeed throughout a career as varied as in IT.

So many organizations put building talent last, because while it seems important, it never seems urgent. Waiting until later is a mistake—especially in technology—and especially in areas such as application development and architecture. Upping the talent in these areas may be the most significant investment you can make.

Imagine what would happen if you did. The most talented workers would be more motivated; other talented technologists would want to join in on the fun. You might need a fraction of your current workforce to accomplish the same objectives.

As you look at the capabilities your organization needs, consider the core technology skills. But at the most senior levels, consider other, arguably more important, capabilities, such as building vision, organizing chaos, communicating effectively, and solving problems.

So look at the whole picture, identify what gaps are most important to close, based on your strategy, and then get the right people in the organization and grow them to their potential. Training and coaching, along with targeted on-the-job growth opportunities, will put employees on a path of excellence. A true focus on this will make a difference in getting each person in the organization focused on improving.

One more word about getting the right people in your organization: You will likely need to clean house, and it will be painful. Unfortunately, your HR department may not support efforts to substantially change the organization. It may not be easy, but it is too important to succumb to the constraints that are hurting so many companies out there. Cleaning house will please your high performers and provide you the space and culture to attract more of them.

Organizational Challenge 3: Structure—Get Out of Your Box!

Often, despite all of the calls for "lean" or "flat" organizations, a massive amount of hierarchy exists. Good ideas rarely flow down through the layers of a hierarchy, and they almost never flow up. Even with overly hierarchical structures, the accountabilities and responsibilities for technology within many organizations are unclear. One would expect hierarchy to make accountability more obvious (in fact, accountability is often the stated reason for authoritarian structures), but the various isolated groups within these hierarchies frequently just point at each other and blame one another for the lack of progress. To fix these problems, isolated groups draw tight lines around what they will be held accountable for so that they cannot fail. And that leaves huge gaps.

In addition to all the hierarchy and accountability issues, we have seen some downright silly organizational structures in our time. There's always a good "reason." Read through these and see if you think we stole any of these ideas from your organization:

"That business unit won't work with anyone but Sally, so we separated out her group."

"Sammy is the only one who understands our system, so we gave him a CTO title and no responsibility to try to keep him."

"We bought this company ten years ago and have just never incorporated them—they operate better independently."

"Grace is the only one I trust, so I have most everything important report to her."

These reasons are accepted as constraints to any organizational changes. Instead of operating within these kinds of constraints, for just a minute, pretend you were starting over. Reboot. Pretend you had the opportunity to design the perfect leadership team and hire people to run those organizations. From scratch. You get to pretend you are David. Seriously, pretend for a minute.

Would you start by thinking about what specialties you would need to execute on your strategy? That's what the Davids are doing across the world right now. Maybe you want mini-CIOs who would support each of your very decentralized business units to get products to market faster. Maybe you want a new head of innovation. Maybe you want flexible development teams that could be applied to

various challenges depending on priorities. Whatever you want likely does not match your current organizational structure or even the talents of your executive team.

After reading that last sentence, you have probably returned to being "reasonable," thinking about all the reasons your organization is structured the way it is today. You probably would rather have much smaller changes. You'd rather be more careful. But hold on a minute. The reason executives often bring in consultants to help design their organizational structure is that we question the obvious and push. There is no reason you cannot do the same.

Companies are structuring technology teams in increasingly creative ways with less and less hierarchy. They have to if they want to survive. While there is no one-size-fits-all approach, there are proven organizational designs for getting products to market faster, for generating more innovative ideas, for strategically sourcing to optimize costs and for bringing in fresh thinking. Proven best practices for organizational design also exist, but we brush them aside because of perceived capability constraints or our limited perception based on how it has always been.

Technology organization design is not a trivial decision. Of course we need to optimize spans of control, minimize layers, minimize team size, and clearly establish accountability. Beyond that, needs may be specific to the company's situation, but most companies benefit from centralized infrastructure and operations and somewhat decentralized, usually agile-based application development teams. Your organizational structure should support your delivery model. For example, your structure will look very different if you are moving toward agile development processes than if you are running a waterfall shop. And your delivery model must support the technology stack you want to build.

More important, every organizational design decision must be tested against the overall strategy to ensure it is helping, not hurting, the effort to achieve strategic objectives. Only after the optimal organizational structure has been designed, and only then, should you start looking at the capabilities of your existing team and determining how to move toward this optimal organization in reality by putting names in those boxes.

We know one thing for sure. These organizational challenges are impeding your company's ability to compete, much less innovate. Organization can either be the anchor that holds your boat back or the sail that captures the wind and carries you forward. The question is—what are you doing about it?

Conclusion

And there it is, the Model we fondly call "the four things." And now that you have made it through this chapter, you may be wondering how best to apply these ideas in your business.

In doing so, you may be concerned that our issues and solutions, although opinionated and sometimes controversial, were relatively broad. We did not provide a checklist of potential issues or recommendations. Strategy doesn't work like that. The specifics are unique to every company and every situation. If you go through a project and use this Model, you will need to get a lot more specific. Just to get your juices flowing, here are some very specific issues and recommendations lifted from recent client reports:

Issues:

- No one (including senior executives) can articulate the technology strategy.
- The culture of the organization is "order taker" versus "strategic leader."
- There are no externally facing systems currently under development, despite the fact that several upstart competitors offer solutions that our clients are already using.
- Application clutter abounds, especially with glorified Access databases supporting finance and sales.
- The development process has too many controls during the design and development phases, but needs better gating before project launch and deployment.
- Business divisions require more decentralized focus, a need which could be served through dedicated business analysts.

Recommendations:

- Transition the VP of application development into a CTO role to better leverage his technology visioning skills. Hire an application development VP to focus on delivering projects and communicating with internal and external stakeholders.
- Create a new sales support organization to focus expertise on customer acquisition, while reducing distraction from core application development resources.
- Retire all CIS applications but one, by moving the others immediately to the India operation and stopping all enhancements.
- Centralize the project-intake process within the enterprise architecture group.

Every single project is different, even though we see similar challenges across our clients. The broad issues and recommendations presented previously are more to orient you to the Model than they are intended to be a practical checklist.

Another concern you might have is where one of your favorite topics fits into the Model. Maybe you are wondering whether performance measurement is a strategy thing or an organizational thing, or whether assigning roles and responsibilities is an organizational thing or a delivery method thing, or whether developmental tools should be analyzed in the delivery method or as part of technology, or whether your technology roadmap is a technology thing or a strategy thing …STOP!

Unless you just love these types of mind games, it's a waste of energy. The Model is just a framework to help you cover your bases, and as long as you cover your topic somewhere, you should rest easy. Remember, it's simply a way to organize thought so that you can innovate more quickly and compete with David. Don't make it complicated by trying to perfect it.

Before we leave the Model, there is another way in which it can be helpful. As we discussed earlier in this chapter, the Model helps us think through the major categories of issues and solutions associated with technology strategy. But, it also helps us think through *dependencies* between these categories.

Businesses are likely to have challenges in all four areas, but the challenges are more likely to be significant in only one or two areas. So where do you begin? You may not want to determine how your organization is structured until you know what kind of technology you are going to build, buy, or support. You may not want to start planning technology until you have the right organization in place.

By default, we always begin with strategy. We usually start by getting clear on the strategy and then evaluating the technology that is needed to support it. Once the technology is understood, the best delivery method to get to that technology can be outlined. Finally, we consider the best organizational structure and associated capabilities required to support that delivery method. In reality, we are looking at all four areas at once and just making hypotheses in that order, continuing to iterate through the four areas.

In the real world, practical considerations often trump theory. For example, if you are trying to decide whether to buy or build a new sales force management system, don't change the organization responsible for delivering it until you've figured out the technology. If you are doing a pilot project testing agile techniques, delay major hiring and training and restructuring until you know whether you are going to stick with your waterfall method or move to agile. If you think you may need to sell off one of your business units, don't force that business unit into a new centralized delivery method and pooled-application development organization. If you are waiting to find out from corporate whether or not you are merging your technology group with several other technology divisions next week, don't pick a system just focused on your division this week.

Just don't let the dependencies freeze you. That's the tendency. It can seem so overwhelming. Consider all the theoretical and practical input and then figure out what you *can* do. Test the best hypothesis of where to begin. Consider the whole system. Remember, that's what David is doing with his new set of tools. He might have the advantage of speed, but you can capture the advantage of organized thought.

Although having a good Model for organizing thought is critical, often the key to transformational innovation requires a powerful approach. Old Goliath companies impede innovation by focusing on risk mitigation and right versus wrong. Great companies, those that use technology to compete, blow up the sacred cows and pet projects in the way they approach innovation. They inspire an innovative spirit, by encouraging the rank and file to try new ideas without fear of retribution from above.

It's now time to reboot the Approach to evaluating and testing the many options available to your company to transform your company's ability to compete.

CHAPTER 5

APPROACH

SCIENCE AS A COMPETITIVE WEAPON

Inside the whiteboard jungle that makes up many businesses, people often demonstrate an approach to new ideas and strategic thinking that is more about avoiding embarrassment than generating and improving ideas. Perhaps this fear of being wrong is just a basic human behavior—a behavior that is reinforced by our educational system and most corporations, nonprofits, and government entities. But regardless of its source, many people are restrained and inhibited by a corporate culture that punishes them when they are "wrong" and rewards them when they are "right" (or at least "not wrong"). Promotions and praise come to the rule-followers, many of whom ultimately end up leading companies.

This kind of culture is pretty useful for avoiding risk. And certainly, there are many roles in organizations where it makes sense to be extremely careful and to avoid making mistakes. However, a culture of "avoiding mistakes" reduces the chance that *anyone* will take risks or make bold decisions. The bolder the risk, the more likely the failure, and the more likely that there will be personal consequences. Over and over, we have seen good ideas squashed before they are even aired because the person with the idea has been burned one too many times and now refuses to speak up (or worse yet, has been trained not to generate the idea in the first place).

When this happens—when the constituents inside the organization hunker down and refuse to share their ideas with the rest of the organization—the organization quite literally loses its ability to think. It cannot generate new thoughts because these thoughts are stifled before they ever get shared. The result? A lack of innovation, which is happening to those Goliath companies that are failing every day.

Before technology, speed became a competitive differentiator; stifled innovation was tolerable. Businesses had fewer problems to solve and more time to solve them. They did not have a slew of global Davids breathing down their necks and stealing their customers overnight.

Those days are over.

We've talked throughout the book about Goliath companies that cannot keep up with the idea generation and execution of their competitors. We see it over and over again in businesses. Most businesses know about this pain point, but question the solution to the pain. Is there a way to improve the generation, vetting and implementation of ideas inside organizations? We think there is. We call it the Approach, and it begins with a guy named Karl Popper.

In 1963, Karl Popper revolutionized science with his groundbreaking publication, *Conjectures and Refutations*. Until this time, scientists generally endeavored to find universal laws in the spirit of the ancient Greeks. They sought, through repeated observations, to distill a law that would explain how some particular part of the universe worked. In this view of science, these laws were discovered in much the same way ship captains discovered new continents and astronomers discovered new planets.

In practice, these "discovered" laws did not hold up for long. For example, the ancient Greeks proposed that the world was made of four indivisible components: earth, air, fire, and water. It didn't take long for even unsophisticated techniques to determine that each of those was divisible into elements. Later scientists divided them into molecules, and then atoms, then subatomic particles, and they continue to divide them today. Each time a scientist tried to claim that his view of the indivisible constituents of matter was the real version, a new scientist with new theories overthrew him. The theory of what composed the world continued to change as more people successfully proved previous theories wrong.

Popper challenged the methodology of his peers. He claimed that there was no such thing as a law in science. There are no laws, and they are not discovered. Instead, he believed that science was an iterative approach to human knowledge. Basically, science encourages the creation of hypotheses (often called theories) and then encourages concerted attempts to prove those hypotheses wrong.

Thus re-envisioned, science is not really a discipline of discovery, but one of creation—creation of hypotheses that, over time, continue to move closer and closer to reality. Science is the process of making a conjecture about how something works and then trying to refute it. Each tentative solution is tested and retested until a new more realistic solution is proposed. The basic activity of science is to do this over and over again in order to get more credible results each time. Popper stated this view in a simple rule: "We progress in science by stating falsifiable claims and then seeking to prove them wrong."

The idea of *falsifiability* has become central to the modern scientific method. A scientific statement now isn't really considered *science* unless it can be argued with, disputed and (crucially) proven wrong. Perhaps a strategic initiative in businesses should not really be considered *strategic* unless it can be argued with, disputed and (crucially) proven wrong? We think so.

Popper's ideas have found their way into many realms of human endeavor, including mathematics, government, and art; but they are not widely known in the business world. And yet, the strategic projects in which business leaders must engage are analogous to the concept of hypotheses Popper proposes in science: each new initiative corresponds to a hypothesis of what will make the company stronger. Each new capability is built with the belief that it will make the business more likely to win. Just as in science, each of these theories is tested. Some of them work in the real world and some of them don't.

This reformulation of the method of science revolutionized the world of scientific thought, and if positioned carefully in today's business landscape, it can dramatically change the way we approach strategic thinking. Popper's method has become the generally accepted method of the scientific community worldwide, and that is reason enough to consider applying these ideas to technology and business.

Strategic initiatives in business function very much like experiments in the scientific community. And thinking about them in this way can help us adopt those initiatives that are most likely to yield good results in the long run. Virtually all organizations that seek to change and grow out of their existing problems can be looked at in this way. Moreover, this Approach to thinking can offer significant benefits for building technology strategies.

An Old and Different Approach

Compared to the way most businesses operate, Popper's approach to strategic thinking is strikingly different. In many organizations, individual leaders come up with strategic plans and then defend them vigorously against criticism (with swords and shields if necessary). They attach their worth in the organization to their strategies. They do everything in their power to promote them.

Popper recommends a significantly different approach in which we look at our own strategies dispassionately and build an organizational culture that focuses on delivering the best criticisms of these ideas as early in the process as possible. How different is this from the way your organization runs?

To make Popper's concepts a bit easier, we've simplified his ideas and incorporated them into the three phases of our Approach: *problem definition, hypothesis creation,* and *tests and refinements.*

Phase I: Problem Definition

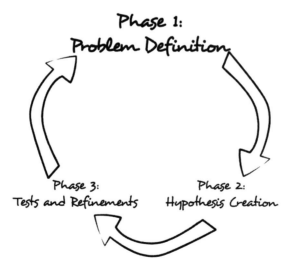

Approach Phase 1: Problem Definition

The first phase of this Approach to thinking is *problem definition.* Success in determining a good strategy (and later implementing that strategy) is built on a foundation of good problem definition. A well-constructed, and clearly stated, problem definition will result in better strategic solutions that will come more easily.

Defining the problem can be difficult. Each issue interrelates with the others to form a very complex environment. Every person in the organization will come to the discussion of strategy with different preconceived notions about the nature of the problems facing the business. People disagree not only about the priority of different problems but about which problems are really problems. Without clear problem definition, the solution will remain murky.

For example, the sales department of a business may see a competitor's latest technology as a threat to its ability to close deals with new customers. At the same time, the CFO of the same organization may be looking at several expensive line items for technology innovation in the budget and may see the problem as high technology costs. The CIO may be concerned about too many different kinds of solutions built on too many different kinds of technology. The strategic problem for the business may be any of these issues or perhaps a combination of any or all of them. If the actual problems are not clearly laid out, documented, and discussed, significant wasted effort in well-intentioned problem solving is likely to occur.

Many thinkers have attempted to create fail-safe recipes for problem definition with little success, but we do have a few guidelines to share that should help.

First, *write the problem down.* We use the Model discussed in the previous chapter to organize our thoughts. (Is this a technology problem? Is it a delivery problem?) The problem has to be written down so it can be discussed, agreed upon, and later reviewed to test whether proposed strategies can solve it. The words do matter. You may need to rethink and rephrase a problem repeatedly to get at its real root. Writing the problem out clearly also removes some of the politics associated with strategic thinking because a written problem statement can be challenged and criticized, disassociated from the person who formed it.

Second, *think at different levels.* Maybe you thought the problem was declining sales, but when you looked at the problem from a broader perspective, you discovered that declining sales were a symptom of a bigger problem—perhaps a lack of innovation or bad customer service. You can also think smaller. Maybe you thought the problem was declining sales, but when you looked at the problem from a narrower perspective you discovered that sales issues were just a symptom of a relatively minor issue—for example, customers were unable to find your website because it wasn't being advertised properly. A clearer definition of the declining sales problem will help to determine the best solution. To clarify the problem, try to think both broader and narrower to assess whether you are defining the problem at the best level.

Third, *continue to ask* (over and over and over again), "What is the problem we're trying to solve?" The context you are operating in may change. And, it is easy to get distracted by other kinds of data or minor issues. So this question cannot be asked too frequently. Sometimes, simply asking it again will sharpen focus on the issues. We often find that asking this question repeatedly throughout a project will yield different results. In other words, the problem we began working on has changed as we've conducted more analysis and learned more. We have seen the merits so we've stopped rolling our eyes or glaring at our well-meaning team member/interrogator when he or she asks for the fortieth time, "Now what problem are we trying to solve?"

Phase 2: Hypothesis Creation

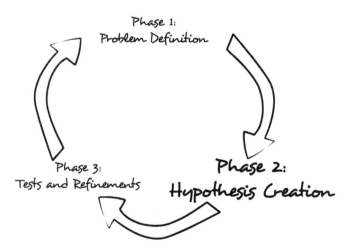

Approach Phase 2: Hypothesis Creation

Once the problem has been clearly defined, the next step is to form a hypothesis that could solve the problem, in a way that allows the ideas to be criticized. This approach is a major change from the way strategies are formed in most organizations where they are frequently so deliberately vague that they cannot be disputed. The Popperian approach to strategic thinking requires that the hypothesis must be able to be proven wrong.

We've heard many business leaders offer vague platitudes in lieu of a real strategy:

- Our strategy is to grow.
- Our strategy is to increase revenue.
- Our strategy is to decrease costs.
- Our strategy is to improve our reputation.

We've discussed throughout this book the risks of these nebulous, banal generalities. It is hard to argue with any of them; and therefore, they are not valid hypotheses for strategies. The central tenet Popper teaches is that if it can't be argued—if it can't be *falsified*—then it isn't science. It also isn't strategy. These kinds of statements most definitely will not get to the desired solution, which is to recognize the most effective strategic initiative and quickly move on it.

Creating a hypothesis requires rewording each statement into something that promotes strategic thinking and analysis.

- Our strategy is to grow *by ten percent by selling our existing products to a new market.*
- Our strategy is to increase revenue *by twenty percent by selling new innovative products to our existing customers.*
- Our strategy is to decrease costs *by thirty percent by offshoring fifty percent of our development.*
- Our strategy is to grow our reputation *by creating a network of websites and blogs that reinforce our central messages so that we will increase the likelihood of gaining new customers.*

Each of the above statements is a real "strategy hypothesis." (Note: We are using the strategy area of the Model as an example, but you would usually have one or more hypotheses within each of the four areas of *strategy, technology, delivery method,* and *organization.*)

These are real hypotheses because you can argue with each. You can say that it is impossible to "grow by ten percent" in this new market and give reasons. You can say that twenty percent of customers won't buy the new product and show some analysis of customers. You can argue that offshoring costs have risen and the company won't be able to reduce development costs by thirty percent. You can debate whether creating websites and blogs will improve the company's reputation in the marketplace.

You may have noticed something in the above strategic hypotheses: three of them have specific measurable goals. Although not strictly necessary, having a measurable statement of how much something will change, makes for even stronger statements. At times it may be difficult to set measurable criteria (like when you are measuring something intangible like "reputation"), but even here there are potential options. For example, "We will have eight out of ten positive hits on a Google search for our product," or "We will have eighty percent positive brand recognition in public surveys."

The fourth example above also illustrates a primary way to clarify a problem, which is to state the reasoning behind it. Although it doesn't specifically lay out a measurement (they are not always available), it answers a key question: "So what?" or "For what result?" It specifically states that the reason the company is engaging in a particular strategy is to "increase the likelihood of gaining new customers." Asking "so what" repeatedly when clarifying a problem ensures that you get to the root of the problem you are trying to solve.

The key point is to specifically design a strategic statement so that it can be criticized. This alone will give your organization an edge. Most companies are quick to criticize, but that criticism is often used against the organization, rather than as a means to help create an advantageous position in the competitive marketplace. Our notion is this: turn that propensity to criticize into a tool. Make it part of your methodology and encourage critical thinking in a constructive way.

One technique for increasing the value and quantity of hypotheses is based on an idea from another scientist: Linus Pauling. He once said, "The way to get good ideas is to get lots of ideas, and throw the bad ones away." During this hypothesis-creation phase, it often helps to start by generating multiple potential hypotheses rather than the one perfect one. We've all seen it work—someone will come up with a totally off-the-wall idea, and we feel like we are going down a rabbit hole until that sparks an idea in someone else that makes us all go, "Hmmmm …"

Many of us know this technique as brainstorming. It is one of the first techniques any manager learns. Usually employed in workshops, this process separates idea generation from idea criticism. As with many business management fads, people tire of anything that is repeated too often, but this approach has held on (despite resistance) for a reason: it works. Brainstorming allows many ideas to be generated because, by separating idea generation from criticism, it turns off the parts of the people's brains that are focused on criticizing and being criticized for a few short, but valuable, moments.

This separation is key when building a technology strategy. This process can be handled formally in brainstorming workshops or more informally by setting up time for new-idea generation. Make the process easy. Your focus should be on creating difficulty for the competition, not for your own organization.

Phase 3: Tests and Refinements

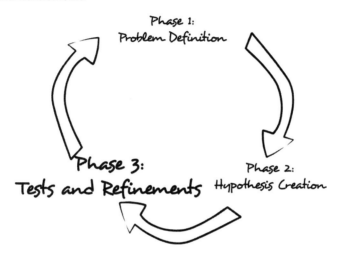

Approach Phase 3: Tests and Refinements

Once your hypotheses are developed, detach from them and open the floodgates of criticism. Hypotheses may be criticized with specific facts or through subjective discussion; either are valuable and help you dispute or refine your hypotheses. If you aren't desperately hoping for criticism at this point, you don't have David's hunger for success. Only through this criticism will your hypotheses turn into strong recommendations, and only then will your business transform into a competitive force.

The first round of testing of hypotheses in any business will generally take the form of some kind of analysis and criticism of the ideas, and this need for criticism brings up a cultural challenge.

Encouraging criticism is a significant change from the way most businesses operate today. This approach may require retraining for many people who have been trained to state things in ways that cannot be criticized to avoid being attacked. Remember, your competition does not care how long it takes your organization to work out these kinds of hindering details.

Don't get attached to ideas

Business people love to get attached to their ideas. People fight, cry, whine, scream, lie, and cheat to protect their personal vision for the strategy of an organization. Something in all of us wants to see our idea be successful or to see our strategy get implemented. Of course, this attitude isn't all bad: people should care about the outcomes. Organizations are designed to offer recognition and advancement for people with successful ideas; however, people shouldn't be attached to their ideas at all costs. All too often, emotional attachment to ideas can cause leadership to pursue the wrong strategy. That is good news for David, who is still young and open-minded. Goliath is slaying himself.

To develop good strategies, hypotheses must be subjected to strong criticism and testing. They must be questioned, challenged, and debated. This process of critical analysis can be emotionally taxing if you can't let go of your pet idea. Each criticism (no matter how factual) will cause an emotional reaction, and you'll find that you are likely to defend an idea even after it has been shown to be ineffective.

This inability to adjust thinking even when new facts are presented causes people to press on with mistakes even after they have been proven to produce unintended negative consequences. When senior leaders get defensive about their ideas, effective criticism is destroyed across the organization. The key is a cultural attitude of submitting to evidence rather than to expectations. It is giving up the hubris attached to a particular idea.

Criticize through debate and analysis

Once we let go of our emotional attachment to particular ideas, we can allow ourselves to execute the key part of this phase: criticism. Every hypothesis for a strategy must be subjected to criticism and testing. Counter to most of what goes on in organizations, everyone (especially the proponent of an idea) must critically examine each hypothesis and try to prove it wrong.

Not having a "critical" culture can lead to significant consequences:

- Organizations waste time and effort on initiatives that were misguided in the first place.
- Organizations incur "opportunity costs" for not pursuing other, more promising initiatives.
- Organizations catch mistakes later in the process when they are more expensive to correct.

The entire team must actively look for evidence that the hypothesis is not meeting (or will not meet) its goals. Most of us look for evidence that it will. We focus on all of the data that supports our case. Of course, we should compile this data, but more important, we should look for the flaws in our idea, the weaknesses and shortcomings.

At the same time, everyone involved in the strategic-thinking process should be mindful to present his or her ideas and criticisms with kindness. Personal attacks and bullying are not only counter-productive, they can shut down attempts at fostering a culture of innovation. In short, transformation will fail if the people involved in the process cannot learn to criticize ideas rather than each other. Imagine what little would have been discovered by those early pioneers if their style of thinking had been restrained and inhibited the way it sometimes is today? Encourage people to get involved in this process as quickly as possible. Remind people that the consequence of failing to transform is that your competition will win.

Two primary methods exist for criticizing strategic hypotheses before they turn into recommendations: debate and analysis. Each has advantages and disadvantages, and each is most useful in certain situations.

Debate is the process of verbally arguing and challenging an idea. It involves thorough discussion of an idea with a focus on uncovering any problems with it. When a team gets really good at working together to critically think through ideas, debate can be a powerful tool for removing bad strategies and for fixing problems with good ones. However, debate must be used with caution because it can lead people to take sides, and once again, become attached to a particular idea.

Analysis is the critical assessment of data. It involves breaking down the strategic idea into its assumptions and looking for data that can be used to validate or dispute it. For example, the strategy hypothesis may say that a business can gain twenty percent market share by introducing a new product, but if the data shows that new products have never garnered more than a ten percent market share, you may conclude that you have a problem with your strategy. (It is also possible that there is something different about this particular product, but at least you have identified an area for discussion.)

Analysis can be completed during the initial stages of strategic thinking, during implementation of a strategy and after the strategy has been implemented. It is at its most powerful when organizations build criticism as a key process from the beginning.

These kinds of tests (criticizing an idea before it "goes live") are relatively cheap and easy. If you can catch the problems early, you can either throw out bad ideas and move on or do something to correct the problem. Abandoning a failed initiative before it begins should be celebrated. Congratulate each other on testing the idea and deciding to move on. Most organizations tend to bury the evidence of failed hypotheses, even though they should be considered successes. Internal politics and personal insecurities don't allow discussion of these failings because they will be perceived as personal weaknesses. Becoming an organization that can deliver on strategic ideas over and over again requires a change in the way criticism is delivered.

Test "In the Wild"

The other kind of test that strategic initiatives go through is "in the wild." In other words, strategic initiatives eventually have to be selected and implemented. Something real has to be done with them. As soon as an idea is put into practice, we can begin watching for feedback on how the idea is working in reality. The same kinds of principles of analysis and criticism apply. Is the initiative having the expected results? What does the data say? Is the project going according to plan?

Once again, normal organizational behaviors can interfere: there is one thing that project managers learn early—avoid telling bad news. If a strategic initiative was supposed to increase revenue by twenty percent, but it is failing to do so, the organization will often conveniently acquire organizational amnesia and forget the original goal. In fact, in most organizations, an in-progress initiative will never be scrutinized again like it was during the approval phase.

We must overcome these cultural barriers. People must be given the room and the encouragement to bring up concerns without being labeled a "negative Nelly." The right context must be created for people to do this. Project status meetings focused on convincing everyone a project is in the "green" must be replaced with meetings where internal issues and outside risks are aired and resolved.

Putting It All Together

The Model and Approach are each useful on their own, but when used together, they are even more powerful in creating an organization that can use speed to compete. The Model organizes thought. A creative way to think of it is as a set of boxes or containers for problems and solutions. The Approach guides the thinking process as you are filling up those boxes. You can think of it as a guide to help generate and refine your thoughts.

Let's look at these two key components in practice by going back to David's lemonade stand, a few years later.

David was very successful. As you recall, when he was only twelve, he launched his first lemonade stand. Now, at twenty-seven, he is one of the richest people in the United States. His little lemonade stand has evolved into an online training portal that now educates over 20,000 kids every summer on how to run their own profitable lemonade stand. Not only is his business highly profitable, David is using the business to teach thousands of kids how to run their own businesses. David is pretty happy.

But he's also worried. He's noticed a lot of competitors trying to take his position. They are offering new products, including a book to appeal to the parents of children who want to start lemonade stands. They are also taking advantage of new technology capabilities, specifically mobile platforms.

Consequently, they are out-innovating David. His organization was once quick to the challenge, but lately they have been behind on every new opportunity. Just today, he learned that a critical project that he thought he'd approved almost a year ago had gotten stuck in a bureaucratic logjam over budget approval. Almost a year later, nothing has been done. Meanwhile, the competition is gaining, while his margins continue to erode.

David decided to get involved in the technology strategy of his organization again. He began with the "four boxes" from the Model and the *problem definition* phase from the Approach. With a couple of his lieutenants, he completed a quick internal and external analysis to summarize and prioritize the biggest challenges. In the area of *strategy*, he found that he was lacking the innovation speed and capability necessary to compete in the market, which resulted in a drastic drop in enrollment of new kids in the last two years. His *technology* was out of date. The core program that ran his training portal was the same one he wrote during his third summer running the business. His organization's *delivery method* had slowed down as well. Each new idea was burdened with a set of reviews, documentation, and business cases, making everything slower and more expensive. His *organization* had become so hierarchical and siloed that information was not moving between the groups. His greatest talent went to work for the competition, and the people that remained were pointing fingers at each other. Yes, David was becoming Goliath.

After completing the problem definition phase of the Approach, ensuring coverage of the Model, David now has a good handle on the real challenges he's facing. With the problems clarified, he can use the hypothesis creation phase to envision potential solutions. What if he changed the company's strategy from a solely training standpoint to also include the selling of supplies required to run a successful lemonade stand? What if he branded his lemonade stand methodology and sold mini-franchises to kids all over the world? What if he redirected all his focus to the education market, targeting teachers and other educators?

What if the first thing they did to improve technology was to replace their oldest, most antiquated system, the crown jewel of the organization—the training portal? They could move the portal to a mobile platform, so that kids could learn about how to set up their stand while riding on the bus to and from school. They could expand the functionality to provide on-the-job support and tools so that kids could continue to refine and improve their business throughout the year. What if they redesigned their delivery method to focus on speed and innovation? What if they removed two or three levels from his organization and allowed decisions to be made lower down in the organization?

David can take these ideas to his trusted advisors to *test and refine* (the final phase of the Approach), encouraging criticism and debate, but not before he gathers a set of people who will really challenge him (he has found these people are as hard to come by as a CEO.) They must discuss each idea in turn. For example, can they really afford to shift their strategy away from cost containment to innovation? Can they replace their oldest system without bankrupting the company? Aren't their delivery methods put in place to prevent mistakes, and would changing them increase their risk? What would happen to their controls if they removed some of the levels of their organization?

Of course, David may not do all of these things. Other ideas will come up, and he will have to prioritize. But, by "walking" the Model with the phases of the Approach, David has added some rigor to his strategic thinking. This rigor helps him feel certain he's covered the major issues and that he is headed forward. He's moving, likely in a good direction, which is much better than frozen in his tracks or hiding in his cave. He's acting more like himself, less like Goliath.

In this simple example, we've only discussed a problem or two in each box of our Model. Of course, in the real business world, issues will be much more numerous and complex. There will be many problems in each box of the Model and some problems (and solutions) will cross into multiple boxes. Problems and hypotheses will rarely be one to one, and the testing process won't simply be a single meeting. Deeper analysis will be required in each of these areas to get to the right problems and solutions.

To manage the complexity of strategic thinking in the real world, to handle all of the interviews, discussions, documentation, team management, and politics necessary to deliver a technology strategy in a real company, we have the final step of the MAP: Project.

In the next chapter, the final piece of the strategy puzzle will be reviewed. The goal is to give your organization a new set of tools as well as help you better leverage tools that are likely already familiar to your organization. To use these new tools, however, you'll need to reboot the way your team executes strategy. You'll have to think like the Davids out there. They have nothing to lose and everything to gain. We'll discuss creating a Project to deliver the strategy. The best part is that if you use these tools, your organization is much more apt to get behind and contribute to your strategy rather than derail your efforts to innovate.

CHAPTER 6

PROJECT

THE ROAD
TO REBOOT

In the last two chapters, we discussed a structured way to organize thinking and an experiment-driven, science-based approach to innovation. Those chapters were, perhaps, a bit theoretical, and you may be looking for more practical steps to organize your team's activities. If so, this is your chapter.

We've found that the best way to organize a technology strategy effort in most companies is through a project. Really, it becomes a *series* of projects carried out in a regular cadence. In fast-moving technology environments, this cadence requires that these projects are undertaken or refreshed as often as quarterly, or at least yearly.

Those who have lived through or witnessed a traditional strategy project in the past, don't panic or toss this book across the room. Not yet. You are probably envisioning a monstrous, six-month to year-long effort that is ultimately outdated and irrelevant by the time it is completed or communicated. Hopefully, you know us well enough by now to know we wouldn't have led you through all the anticipation of a better way of doing things to end up there again. Give us a chance. We don't want to end up on the shelf, either.

The fact is that projects are necessary to give an organization a way to focus efforts on related activities. People can be assigned, dates can be set, deliverables can be laid out, and decisions can be made. Turf challenges can be avoided, the project team can operate with a common mission, and all this makes it easier to communicate across the organization.

Even though we will outline the tools to do it differently, better than in the past, this kind of project is still a big undertaking that will consume much of your time, energy, engagement, and leadership. Your predecessors may have failed at similar undertakings, and the organization may be skeptical of your ability to deliver. The team you assemble will require your help in setting direction and in dealing with ambiguity; and the guidance you give will lead to your success or failure. In an attempt to analyze a variety of situations and issues from all angles, team conversations can easily wander and strategic thinking can go on forever. The team can all too easily wobble around, hit stumbling blocks and lose productivity. The people you will need to rely on to own critical pieces of your strategy project may not know what to do first, second or third, much less how to coordinate those activities among team members.

In short, you'll find that you need a new kind of *project plan.* One that moves you as fast and thoroughly as possible to the outcome you want—inspiration, innovation, and buy-in.

As we all know, a project plan lays out an order of steps necessary to deliver on a set of objectives. We know a project plan helps set schedules and costs, identify key dependencies, and coordinate the project team's activities. We know how important these project plans are for big, lengthy, complex efforts. But do we really need a project plan for a little six- or twelve-week strategy project primarily executed by a couple of people?

Absolutely, but it is a different type of plan with slightly different objectives. There will likely be a core team to coordinate, but that team will probably be smaller, and their objectives and deliverables will be a little more fluid. The natural tendency on these types of projects is to get focused on each of the tasks within the plan, while losing sight of the ultimate objectives. It isn't about the strategic linkage diagram, the technology standards compliance assessment, the technology health diagrams, the elegant and detailed reference architecture, the capability maturity model assessment, the SLA benchmarks, the interlinked process flows, the organizational charts with their spans of control or layers analysis, the RACI diagrams, the cross-referenced skills assessment, the employee engagement survey results, the go-forward values, the detailed project proposals, or the financial analysis. Deep breathe. You get the picture.

Any of those tools may help you get to the answers, but they are just tools. Don't forget that. Don't let your team forget that, either.

What is it about? It is simply about nailing the problems and coming up with the most innovative solutions you possibly can. It is about getting to "violent agreement" with all your stakeholders on what is holding you back as an organization, and then about building and maintaining a vision about how to transform your company.

Now we will overlay some more tactical steps you can take to support the thinking and the processing via the Project. Let's take a look at some specific ideas for structuring the work of a strategy project.

Project Component of the Strategy MAP

As we discussed at a high level in Chapter 3, the basic Project from the Strategy MAP is broken into three steps.

- **Step 1—Assessment:** The assessment includes analyzing your business's external and internal world. In this step, you look at where you are, what you have to work with, what your customers (the real ones) need, and what your competitors are doing. The focus is on a clear, hard-nosed assessment of the current capabilities of the business, its technology, its delivery method, and its organization. You also look out into the world to assess what is changing from a business and technology perspective and identify the opportunities and threats of those changes.

- **Step 2—Vision:** Vision involves the creation of the solution. In this step, you design where you want to be and what you'll need to get there. The hardest creative work of the project is completed here: designing a solution that will fill the strategic needs of the organization. The focus is on bold creativity and transformational design of new solutions. You create a new vision for using technology strategically.

- **Step 3—Plan:** The plan outlines the actions to be taken to deliver the strategic vision. You build a plan (or set of plans) to transform the existing technology, delivery method, and organization into the new vision. The focus is on setting practical steps and measurable criteria for the realization of the strategy. You build a roadmap for the various projects it will take to get to the vision you created. You estimate costs, timelines, and dependencies for each project in your overall plan.

Let's revisit the last chapter for a minute and talk about how the Approach overlays this Project plan. Remember, the Approach is a science-based way to translate problems into hypotheses into recommendations into action.

Each of the steps of the Project is correlated to a phase from the Approach. During the assessment step, we are primarily following the problem definition phase of the Approach. In order to transition between the assessment step and the vision step, *we* follow the hypothesis creation phase of the Approach. In fact, at the end of our assessment, the last slide we usually cover with our stakeholders is a high-level hypothesis validation in order to communicate where we are going next and ensure we are on the right track.

During the vision step, we continue down the path of hypothesis creation, taking the high-level hypotheses and building them out to a level of detail that can really be challenged. The natural transition from there is to initiate the tests and refinements phase, as the team begins to analyze and debate the proposed solutions.

In the final step of the Project, the plan, thinking is primarily focused on tests and refinements from the final phase of the Approach. The discussion and debate around individual business cases and project plans is one level of testing and refinement, and then the ultimate test comes when prioritizing and scheduling the set of projects recommended through an overall implementation plan.

This correlation is not a hard-and-fast rule. Sometimes during the assessment, we create a hypothesis, test it, refine it, and "spin it out" for implementation before the strategy project is even done. Sometimes we identify new problems that need to be defined during the vision or plan step. This data often necessitates tweaks (and occasionally major changes) to the strategy we are creating. The art of it all is to keep focused while remaining open to challenges to previous thinking.

Following a clear plan can keep your team working toward the end goal and prevent too many detours. Generally, it is prudent for the leader of a technology strategy project to insist on executing the process in order. The team will be tempted to leap back and forth between phases; and although some churning can be beneficial, overdoing it will cause delays and frustration.

The exact steps a team will go through will vary each time you undertake a technology strategy project because the problem is different each time. The steps we walk through in this chapter serve as a helpful starting point and can be modified to fit your particular needs.

Before You Begin: Setting the Scope

We've talked about this extensively in the previous chapter, so we won't repeat ourselves too much, but defining the problems that need to be solved is crucial to the success of any strategy project. Consulting firms are not always helpful in this area, for they are eager to start billing, thinking that their cookie-cutter approach will ensure that they define the problem(s) later. They aren't the only ones—we see it with internally initiated efforts, too.

Here's the challenge...or the opportunity. You can use this kind of project to tackle very broad problems like the overall structure of technology decision making in a company or relatively small problems related to planning specific products offered in a specific market. Whatever the scope, the key to success is to define a clear problem and consider what dependencies must be included in the analysis.

Without a clear problem and scope, it is too easy to begin by collecting all kinds of data that will eventually be irrelevant. Unclear problems yield unclear deliverables that no one will read or care about. Setting the problem and scope clearly will enable the team to move quickly. Many of these projects can be delivered in six to eight weeks if the problem is clear and the team is focused. In fact, doing these projects quickly is crucial to maintaining focus. Strategic projects that drag on and on become a frustrating waste of time for all involved.

Determining how long a project needs to run is a relatively simple exercise, and we won't insult your intelligence by telling you how to estimate a project—we assume you've probably had to estimate many projects in your past if you are reading this book. It's a (theoretically) simple exercise of figuring out how much work you have to do (how many interviews you need to conduct, how many workshops you have to run, how much data you need to collect, how much writing and thinking time you need, etc.) and how many people you have on your team who can do it. As with all projects, it is best to leave yourself some wiggle room to ensure that you can flex as you encounter surprises along the way.

Project Step 1—Assessment

This may seem like a simple, perhaps even valueless step. You already know your organization—it's your business after all. You know your customers. You know your markets. You know your technology. You know your processes.

Or do you?

Most of the time, the organization *does not know* itself clearly. Any single person really cannot understand modern organizations with all of their associated size and complexity in detail. Furthermore, organizations change regularly, so knowing how a particular part of the organization behaved three years ago may be almost irrelevant today—particularly if technology is involved. Perhaps someone in the organization knows its customers, markets, technology, and processes. Maybe someone understands the competition. And someone else knows what is selling. But these are rarely the same person, and chances are, they don't talk. They may not even know each other.

In other words, the organization doesn't know itself, although its constituent parts might know pieces. The assessment step gives the team the opportunity to gain insights from the right people inside and outside the organization, to research and to deliberately analyze the current state of the business. The assessment step gives you that critical time to pull everything together. Most critical is the opportunity to gain agreement among stakeholders as to what the most pressing problems are that need to be addressed. That's what people miss when they don't do an assessment—the chance to really get the problem definition phase of the Approach right.

The people who do this kind of work well, who have a real talent for creating insightful assessments, approach the problem with the spirit of a detective. They are not simply interviewing, researching, and gathering data. They look at the data as if it were a puzzle they are trying to put together, constantly taking in each new piece of information and asking, "So what does this tell us? What does this data tell us about our situation? How does it change our perspective?" Thinking back to the Approach again; they are working on problem definition and starting to drive toward hypothesis creation.

Cultivating the approach of a detective reminds us that we must aggressively uncover and voraciously consume as much data as we can. It reminds us that insights can come from the smallest details and, perhaps more important, that seemingly unconnected details can be put together to tell a perceptive story. This is why having the broad perspective and insight of a team (instead of trying to do this as a single individual) during the assessment is so critical.

During the assessment, the team should be studying everything it can get its hands on. The exact list of material for review will depend on the scope of the strategy, but may look something like the following:

- Previous and current business strategy documents
- Previous and current technology strategy documents
- Current initiatives and projects underway
- Application inventories
- Architecture diagrams
- IT governance processes
- Project delivery methodologies
- Organization charts
- Skills assessments

The team should also prepare for and conduct as many discussions as it reasonably can in the time allotted:

- C-level executives
- Business unit leads
- Technical experts
- Salespeople
- Marketing
- Customers
- Support staff (e.g., HR and finance)

Finally, the team should observe and analyze the external environment, including:

- Competitors
- Suppliers
- Customers
- Technology trends
- Industry reports

All of this data will begin to come together as the team sifts through the material looking for patterns, inconsisten-

cies, and insights. During the analysis of each of these pieces, the team is reaching for understanding and seeking the answer to the question, "So what does this tell us?" Good detectives may start with a relatively broad set of questions when interviewing and gathering documents; but as they quickly refine their understanding of the problems, they will adjust interview questions and ask for different follow-up documentation.

At the end of the assessment, the goal is to have your current state fully understood by your team and its stakeholders. That understanding must include a clear, concise agreement as to the problems (and opportunities) the organization faces.

As with any given strategic problem and any given team, there will be an optimal way of organizing the work of that team to deliver the best results. Generally, the tried-and-true method proven by project managers for decades is to create interim deliverables, assign responsibilities, and monitor deadlines. This approach works on strategy projects as well, in all three steps, assessment, vision, and plan.

This kind of deliverable-focused team management helps the team work better together, ensures that all of the key areas of investigation are covered, and (if deliverables are carefully reviewed by the team) helps deliver the resulting answers to questions asked along the way. By forcing the team to write down its results along the way and to ask the "so what does this tell us" question, you can substantially improve the thinking that goes into the next phase.

The deliverables from the assessment will look something like the following, which will closely follow the four areas of the Model:

- External trends and opportunities (market, regulatory, technology)
- Current business and technology strategy (if they exist)
- Current technology set
- Current delivery methods
- Current organizational analysis
- Issues and opportunities clearly laid out for each area

This short list is simply a starting point for the list of deliverables you'll want to find or create in this phase. Numerous tools (like SWOT analyses, RACI charts, governance charts, competitive assessments, customer satisfaction surveys, architecture diagrams, technical health charts, and many others) may work in your organization to document some of these areas.

The real key is to make sure there is adequate coverage and that each section of the assessment deliverable is produced in the spirit of the detective. What does it mean that our business strategy isn't clear? What does it mean that our organization is hierarchical? What does it mean that our top competitor just launched into a new market space? What does all this tell us?

The assessment step concludes when the team has a good feel for the strategic challenges the organization is facing. You'll know you are done when you have a short but punchy report that provides insights on problems and opportunities and leads toward hypotheses of solutions. All the analyses will back up this summary. The team should review this assessment with a group of senior leaders who can challenge the analysis. This step is critical because not only does this criticism of the assessment improve the results, but it also gets the senior team on board with the direction of the strategy. If you can get the organization to agree to the problems now, you are more likely to get them to agree to the solutions later.

Project Step 2—Vision

Now comes the hard part, but it is the most fun for those of us geeks who thrive on this stuff. Now that we have a clear understanding of the issues and opportunities as well as some initial, high-level hypotheses for how we can exploit them, we get to start envisioning the future.

We've read everything available about what makes a good strategy, how notable strategic thinkers think, how companies build successful strategies and how academics think about the subject. If you are a methodology geek, you can find many of them with a quick search on Wikipedia—Balanced Scorecards, Blue Ocean Strategy, Core Competencies, Scenario Planning—the list goes on and on. These are all helpful tools in the right circumstance, but they are *not* the strategy itself. They are means to get to the strategy. There are books on the subject, MBA classes, military strategy classics, hundreds of articles and blogs, and yet, no one seems to be able to answer the simple question of how it is that people come up with strategies that work. What is the spark of insight, or the moment of magic, that prompts excellent strategy?

Strategic thinking is an almost magical combination of knowledge, creativity, insight, drive, and luck that comes together at the right time to yield an excellent vision. We would be lying if we told you we knew exactly how that magical moment happens (as do the so-called gurus who claim they know an exact recipe for strategy).

That said, a few proven techniques increase the likelihood that a motivated team can come up with an excellent strategy. You can create the right kind of environment in which strategies can grow. You can

save yourself and your team from getting buried in the weeds or traveling too far down the wrong path.

To drive innovation, create an environment of innovation. This can be more challenging than one might expect. Fostering inspiration and innovation with your team, including your core team and your stakeholders, is the key that sets apart typical strategy projects from true successes. So humor us as we talk a little about how to lead a team through the ambiguity of this step, then we'll get to some of the more practical pointers about what you actually need to be doing during this step.

Creating an environment of innovation can be difficult because no project team wants to put forward ideas that might be wrong. Teams want to be structured; they want to hit their dates. The structure of most projects is focused on delivering something, *anything,* by a certain time, but even with that focus, it is often during this vision step that projects go off the rails. Those who didn't get drowned in analysis paralysis during the assessment may be overwhelmed by the ambiguity and myriad of alternative ideas generated during the vision.

The person leading the vision step of a project must create the kind of structure that encourages open thinking and brainstorming followed by rigorous (but kind) criticism of those ideas. Hypotheses creation from Phase 2 of the Approach is the primary tool to use at this time. We use the word "hypothesis" very intentionally because it removes some of the attachment to the ideas being generated. It is this hypothesis-centered approach that allows a team to be innovative.

We often start with a group hypothesis activity: take each of the discoveries from the assessment (i.e., problems that need to be solved, markets that should be pursued, strengths that should be exploited) and ask a simple question, "What should we do about this?" It is helpful to enforce an old brainstorming workshop rule of "no criticism" to encourage the generation of ideas. Criticism and priority setting can come later.

Then we divide and conquer to develop individual hypotheses—assigning particular problems to each member of the team and asking them to spend some time individually thinking about and researching solutions. Then we use the team as a sounding board for further criticism, debate, and analysis. Throughout this process, the "team" may be the core project team or a broader group of stakeholders, depending on the problem. Whatever the specific steps, we find that the combination of individual thinking and group thinking yields the most insightful results.

In almost all cases, both the project plan and the resulting deliverable begin with the strategy area of the Model. You must get clarity on the overall strategy before diving into each of the other three areas of the Model, because the strategy will drive your hypotheses around technology, delivery method and organization. This is the primary reason the Approach phases and the Project steps do not align one-to-one. In the strategy area of the Model, you must quickly drive through hypothesis creation and tests and refinements so that you can get to the best hypotheses in the other three areas.

Now that we've talked about how to use a hypothesis exercise to encourage individual and group thinking, let's get back to a more practical discussion of how to develop your vision. As you hypothesize and refine the strategy, remember that the simpler it is, the better. Ideally, this is one slide, or even one short statement. It is whatever high-level direction you need to establish clarity around what technology you need to build, what method will best deliver it, what organization will best support it.

Do you need to constantly drive new innovations within your existing product suite to expand into new customer segments or be prepared to quickly integrate acquisitions of new product lines to provide a full suite of solutions to your existing customer base? That's just an example, but you can envision how those strategies would change the hypotheses around the technology, delivery method and organization.

Once the strategy is established, continue to use the Model to determine which areas you will cover with your hypotheses. Depending on the scope for your project, you may be focusing more in certain areas than others. For instance, if you are primarily focused on the organization area of the Model, the hypotheses will have to do with topics such as where people will report, how you will build capabilities in your organization, etc. They should be as specific as possible, for example:

- We will establish a new business analysis competency, aligning business analysts to each major business unit to build understanding of our customers and markets.
- All technology infrastructures will be centralized into one group and opportunities for out-sourcing portions will be evaluated.
- We will build our own "Tech School" through a combination of internal and external training.

Hypotheses in the technology and delivery method areas will look very different than the organization-related examples above. Whatever the hypotheses, the goal is to refine them so they become recommendations, or alternatively, to "disprove" or deprioritize them.

This step of the Project is the least cookie cutter, so outlining the specific deliverables is unrealistic here; but at the highest level, it will again follow the four areas of the Model:

- Technology strategy
- Future state technology architecture
- Delivery method recommendations
- Future state organizational structure
- Capability recommendations

That's just a high-level starting point for the deliverables you'll want to develop in this phase. Numerous tools (scorecards, reference architectures, technology vendor analyses, governance charts, process maps, RACI charts, capability frameworks, business cases, and financial analyses) may help you as you develop, analyze, challenge, and refine each hypothesis.

In the end, whatever deliverables you create are just support for your individual and group analysis of the hypotheses. They also help document decisions as you move forward, which will be critical later as you engage project managers to execute your plans. By the end of this phase, your team should have a future state vision that describes what your technology, delivery methods and organization will look like after the changes you recommend are implemented.

Project Step 3—Plan

And now, as we enter the last step of our Project, we have bad news for you. Most strategies fail. If there is a breaking point in the success of most strategies, it is here: translating strategy into action. The good news is that, if you do this step right, your chances of success skyrocket.

Sometimes failure is due to a bad strategy or one that isn't well thought through; but even the best-designed, most insightful, most thorough, most revolutionary strategy can easily come to naught when it meets with resistance or a lack of capability to execute. If what you are proposing is something really different, something that will really change the organization (in other words something strategic) then implementing that strategy is going to be challenging.

One of our clients has a bookcase in his office with a complete shelf reserved for the strategy projects of the past. It has twenty to thirty beautiful documents on it. Consultants built many; internal people built some. None, we repeat, none, of these strategies were ever implemented, producing an entire shelf of wasted effort. Unfortunately, this is more common than not; and as you're reading this, you're probably nodding your head in agreement.

It is tempting to blame these failures on the quality of the strategies themselves. Let's face it: some strategy documents are full of useless drivel. Sometimes it appears that someone was just playing around with whatever jargon was popular in their day. Sometimes they appear to be pure academic exercises using the latest frameworks of their time: Enterprise Architecture, Segmentation Strategies, "Good to Great," etc. Often, they simply take some of those good academic concepts as a template and try to "fill it out." Sometimes it appears that someone just copied an old deliverable, replaced some of the content, tried to make it pretty, and called it quits.

It is no wonder that nothing ever happened with those ideas. But, on any shelf, there are a few great ideas sitting there. A few of those strategies (had they been implemented) would have changed the industry. Competitors who came to the same strategy and were able to execute on it, implemented a few of them quite successfully. Brilliant ideas are likely sitting on every IT executive's shelf; but, as our client said, "These are a reminder that even the best ideas will become shelf-ware if I can't figure out how to actually move the organization. Every time I see this shelf, it reminds me to get out of my head, to get out of my ideas and to get something done. What really matters is what we do after the strategy project. What really matters is what we do on Monday morning. What really matters is that we follow through."

We couldn't agree more.

Often this lack of follow-through is because the people doing "strategy work" consider it below their pay grade to wade into actual implementation or because a consulting company built the strategy and didn't help their client transition into action. This is why we recommend an explicit planning step as the final piece of the strategy project. The planning step of your project takes the ideas from the strategy and translates them into specific actions (or projects) with deliverables, dates, responsibilities, budgets, action items, risks, issues, and dependencies.

In other words, you prepare to kick off the projects that will deliver on the strategy. And if the projects are staged for a later kickoff, they need to be defined to the point that a project manager could later pick up the report and have enough background to launch the project.

If you are doing something strategic, something that will really change your business, then the plan will, in large part, determine whether you are successful in delivering. Strategies will transform your technology, delivery methods and organization. And, it is the nature of those technologies, delivery methods, and organizations to resist change.

If you want to inspire and enact change, you better have a good plan—a really good plan. The traditional way of planning remains the most effective: put together a series of discrete projects or initiatives. These projects will be handed off to teams to execute, so you must make them very clear, and you must know what the dependencies are between projects.

We aren't going to take you back to Project Management 101 because we know you are familiar with these types of deliverables; and if not, there are many books to read on the subject of building good, actionable plans, and on measuring results. We'll just highlight the key deliverables that are critical to this step of strategy projects:

- Project overviews
- Implementation plan
- Resource plan
- Financial plan
- Issues and risks analysis
- Control and management

Together, these deliverables constitute the beginning of your plan. The plan is, in many ways, the most important step in the overall strategy. It is here that the strategy is likely to receive its strongest criticism. It is often only at the moment of seeking approval (and, of course, funding) from senior leadership that a strategy really gets a full vetting. Only then will people really speak up.

In order to fund projects, businesses once again criticize the ideas, budgets, risks, and potential returns. This can be frustrating because you wanted this kind of feedback earlier in the process, but so long as you know to expect it, you can be prepared to take the feedback and make adjustments.

Throughout this step of the Project, as you are deep in the tactics of developing the plan that will deliver your strategy and reviewing that with all your stakeholders, we encourage you to step back and consider a simple question:

Will this plan actually deliver the strategy?

It is amazing how often the plan falls short of delivering on the strategy—not because it fails or goes awry, but because the plan never addressed the breadth of projects that would be necessary to create the new vision. *The plan itself fell short.* In other words, the plan did not rise to the level of the strategy.

Once a plan is built and before you move on to execution, it is vital to look once again at the plan to see whether it will really deliver on the strategy. The best way to ensure that we have covered everything necessary to deliver on the strategy is to once again use the Model from Chapter 4. Its four areas can help think through what may be missing.

Strategy

- Is the strategy still clear?
- Can you still argue with the strategy, or did it get blurred during project planning, i.e., Would Karl Popper be pleased?
- Will you know if you've achieved the strategy?

Technology

- Are there plans to make the technology changes necessary to deliver on the vision?
- Are we doing something new with technology? (Does the technology take us in a new direction, or did we end up with a simple list of changes to existing technology?)
- Is the solution creative?

Delivery Method

- Is the way you are working likely to deliver the strategy?
- Where are the biggest risks?

Organization

- Are there plans to make the organizational changes necessary to deliver on the vision?
- Do you have the capabilities to deliver on the strategy?
- Did we avoid hard choices that should have been made?

After this final criticism of the strategy and the plan built to deliver it, there will probably be work to do to shore up holes in the overall plan. Regardless, you are nearing the end of this particular strategy project, and even though there may be future refinements to this strategy, you've completed a huge first step. Take a deep breath, you made it! If you have achieved buy-in on the problems, clarity on the vision

and agreement as to the plan to achieve it, you are well on your way and far ahead of your competitors.

The Strategy MAP is our methodology for executing projects designed to ensure companies are equipped to compete with technology. We believe its use is critical in the midst of the converging technology forces that are forcing Goliath companies to rethink the way they go to market. No longer can companies solely think in terms of implementing systems. Instead, they must think in terms of revolutionizing the way they think about and make decisions around technology. This Strategy MAP is designed to move your organization forward, by organizing thoughts, approaching innovation systematically, and quickly driving to an actionable plan.

Competition. Technology trends. Vision. Strategic plans. These simple words often freeze or endlessly spin organizational thinking. This MAP is simply one way to get unstuck and get moving (quickly) to compete with technology. It is a way for big companies to behave more like David companies and for small companies to be more systematic in their thinking. We think it works. But nothing will come of it if you don't act.

In the final chapter, we describe some of the barriers to defining and implementing strategy and how you can overcome them. Monday morning will be here again before you know it, and we want to make sure you are ready for action.

SECTION 3

PRESS THE REBOOT BUTTON

CHAPTER 7

MONDAY MORNING
A FRESH START

So, are you David or are you Goliath?

Not your company...you.

Do you view the "business" as separate from the IT organization?

If you've made it this far in the book, you probably aren't the kind of leader who goes through the motions and takes orders from "the business." You are seeking meaningful change, and you really want to see your business compete and win.

Perhaps you want to be David, but feel stuck in a two-headed Goliath organization. Or maybe you are lucky enough to be in David organizations now, but sense the impending doom as innovation starts to be slowed by bureaucratic processes. If you didn't grasp it before you picked up this book, it's probably clear to you now that there's a revolution underway, and that real technology strategy could change your business and your industry.

We believe there is a part of every human being that wants to innovate. Our basic human DNA has hardwired us to want to be better—to improve, grow, and expand. Yet, despite that drive in all of us as individuals, most companies have stifled our desire for growth and placed limits on what can be done. Those are the Goliath companies.

A David company sees no limits. It sees only opportunity. So, what do you see inside your company? Limitations or opportunities?

This book provides the basic framework to equip you to lead technology innovation and transformation inside your company to compete in your markets. The Strategy MAP provides the basic tools to arm your company with a technology strategy that will make it a competitive force on the global playing field. And you know your organization must compete using technology or it will die in the midst of global competition.

So what's next? While the problem of Goliath's two heads and David's threatening tool set is clear, and the solutions laid out through the Thought Ensemble Strategy MAP are straightforward, your business's challenges, as well as your company's willingness and ability to tackle these challenges, are unique.

You may still feel stuck, not sure where to begin, or not convinced it will make a difference if you do. Although our goal was to equip and inspire you to conquer these challenges, the reality is that corporate change is never easy. We get it. We've been at this crossroads many times, so we understand the hesitancy. We've seen the repercussions of not taking action immediately, but we have also seen the rewards of moving quickly to capture a first-mover advantage, or the transformation of an entire company or industry through the successful implementation of advancement in technology.

It's always at these times that we tell ourselves (and others) to take a deep breath and dive in.

If you aren't quite ready to dive in, take a moment and think about what would happen if you did. This book has likely sparked some inspiration about how a solid technology strategy could drive change in your organization.

Technology changes so fast it is hard not to have ideas if you pay the least bit of attention to what's happening all around. Customers, *not* investors, are now pushing most companies. They are asking for technological change; companies don't have to push technology to their customers. There's no reason you cannot get out ahead of them and use this revolution to explore some evolution inside your company's walls.

As you think through possibilities, visualize alternative futures for you and your company. Visualize what will happen if you succumb to the two-headed Goliath, making evolution a lower priority than other day-to-day activities. It may feel like the safer, easier route, but it will not end well, for you or your company. Then visualize what will happen if you act like David. Better yet, what if you inspired your entire organization to be a David? What if you used the global threat of competition as a call to arms? What would that look like?

You could drive the innovation engine inside your organization, bringing new ideas to your company and to your industry. It may sound more challenging, but it is likely the only way you or your company can really be successful in the long term. And, as we have learned from the history played out right before us, "long term" nowadays is only a couple of years, maybe. So don't wait until tomorrow.

Let's face it. Transforming into David is the only option. It may seem daunting, but it is way more fun. You and your colleagues will have much more enjoyment and satisfaction along the way playing David instead of Goliath. There's just nothing like creating a vision you believe in and then having a chance to realize that vision.

So, are you game? Do you want to inspire evolution? Do you want to reboot technology strategy?

As you calculate your next move inside your company, here are a few tips to equip you for the journey.

1) It Starts With You

Let's be brutally honest here. Taking on this kind of endeavor is a challenge. If you are going to lead this up, formally or informally, start with a clear vision that motivates you first. The best coaches know that they have to believe they can win the game before they are able to rally others to take on the competition.

To start, put all constraints aside. Dream a little. What could your company and your industry look like in the future? What might the strategy be? What might the technology look like? How would your organization work together more efficiently and effectively? How might your organization look different? What would your role be?

You don't have to have all the answers yet, and in reality, you don't want to have all the answers yet. But, thinking about those questions and having some ideas about inspiring answers will keep moving things forward.

Having a few stories to tell, to inspire people, and honestly to scare them into taking action, will be critical when you are building support.

Envision the possibilities. Get yourself clear. And only then it is time to start enrolling others.

2) Enrolling Others

Strategic change is difficult, if not impossible, to launch as a grassroots effort. If you are reading this book, you are probably already senior in your organization or you hope to be one day. Unless you are the CEO, you likely need to enroll people up the proverbial food chain within your organization to affect change. And if you are in an IT organization, you will need to get some senior business stakeholders on board and involved. You might even buy them a copy of this book and discuss it over lunch or dinner.

One of our first clients at Thought Ensemble was initially just a friend to whom we had been giving advice for months. He saw the need and opportunity for strategic change across his organization but could never quite get the focus from his boss or peers. He called excited one day after having a conversation with the president of his business unit about how many of the organizational changes they were planning needed to be considered in the context of the overall vision, as well as their needed technology and delivery model (in fact, he used our "four things" Model to illustrate his point).

After the first critical conversation with the president where he got vision lock, he worked hard to gain traction with other business execs and his boss, the CIO, to ultimately launch an extremely successful technology strategy project. It had taken months to get the right people truly engaged and on board with the holistic way of thinking, but once he did, he was able to run one of the most successful strategy development and execution efforts we have seen. He engaged people early around the critical need for a cohesive vision and kept them involved at key points throughout the project.

Start building allies early. Find out what possibilities inspire them and show them how this strategy project can help realize those possibilities.

3) The "Whack-a-mole" Game

One of the hardest things about leading a strategy project is dealing with the daily interruptions and distractions that are, or may seem, critical for running your business. We talked about "whack-a-mole" in Chapter 4 as a delivery challenge that holds organizations back. Lisa named this phenomenon a few years back after the arcade game we played when we were kids, where the little moles pop out of their holes, and you pound them with a rubber mallet until they stop.

But they never stop popping out of their holes! Many of our clients literally spend six to ten hours of their days in meetings, and few of those meetings help them achieve their business objectives. Any time not spent in meetings can easily be spent answering emails. Entire days, weeks, and months go by just responding to other people's requests.

Many executives' days look something like this: Wake up, run to the phone to check email. Whack! Talk on the phone with colleagues while driving. Whack! Arrive at work and check email again. Whack! Attend three consecutive meetings. Whack! Whack! Whack! During those meetings, while only half paying attention, respond to another fifteen emails. Whack! Lunch with a colleague. Whack! Three more meetings. Whack! Whack! Whack! Another twenty emails. Whack! An emergency meeting. Whack! And suddenly, the day is gone.

How do you make any kind of strategic progress in the whack-a-mole environment? First, turn it into a game. If you think of your day like a whack-a-mole game, you can try to get better at playing it. And, if you think of it like a game, you can also get better at turning it off. It takes discipline. Numerous studies show that recent technological advances are improving our ability to multitask (i.e., play whack-a-mole) while simultaneously stunting our ability to generate deep thought (i.e., think strategically). But you can if you step away from the whack-a-mole addiction. Set aside time for your strategy every week, if not every day.

4) Constipated Python

Jim once drew a picture of a constipated python on a client's whiteboard. The picture may have been a little disturbing, but that probably wasn't what caused the moment of stunned silence and the ensuing giggles around the room. Once they got over the apparently inappropriate metaphor, he explained: their organization kept coming up with more and more ideas, launching more and more projects, but nothing was coming out the other end. It was a constipated python. They were stuck.

Your organization will get stuck. Your team will get stuck during the development of the strategy, and anyone involved in its implementation will get stuck.

This is the time to remember the hypothesis-driven approach. That's one of our biggest secrets! Basically, whenever someone says that they can't move forward until such-and-such decision is made, we throw out a hypothesis for the decision and suggest moving forward based on that hypothesis alone. The key? *Move forward.* Keep advancing the ball. That's what David companies are doing.

For example, whenever someone says the business needs more detailed analysis, we suggest the answer that is most likely and suggest moving forward. Whenever someone says we have to wait for the results of some other project, we suggest what those results will likely be and suggest moving forward. In other words, we use the hypothesis-driven approach to push when things start to slow down.

Know that there is something deeply uncomfortable about using the hypothesis-driven approach in this way. You will feel pushy and those around you will feel that you are pushy as well. Incidentally, that's why it is critical to enroll allies early in the game. This process forces ideas to be advanced. It also means putting forward ideas that will make people around you uncomfortable. But keep at it because its pushiness is exactly why it is so effective in organizations. This approach gives you a way to confront each slow-down in a project, each potential roadblock, each delayed decision.

The good news is that it gets easier. Whenever someone gets stuck in the "what if" loop, you can ask them, "What is your hypothesis?" And, if they are trained in this method, they will look at you (probably with a pained expression) because they know they have to get out of the loop and make a suggestion. They will get better at using it themselves.

And when a team is trained in this approach and when they have some consistent language in using these ideas, it opens them up to challenging you, too. In other words, they will catch you when you get stuck in your "what if" loop. They will force you to use the technique to make decisions as well.

This technique benefits everyone involved; but more important, it creates a David-like culture that will increase the chances your company can win.

5) Relentless Prioritization

At some point in the process, often early and always toward the end, you and your executive team will want it all. Whether you are just starting your strategy or wrapping it up, if you do it right, you won't be challenged by a lack of ideas. The challenge will be the constraints, usually in the form of financial and human resources, to make all those ideas happen. And really, even if you had unlimited resources, it doesn't make sense competitively to go after everything at once. You simply can't focus on everything effectively.

So you have to prioritize, and your team will fight this tooth and nail. The funny thing is that those who are closest to those constraints are often the ones who have the most trouble prioritizing. This is delusional. Not prioritizing is a sure path to failure.

Someone needs to be the sane one and tell people "no" and that they are likely to fail if they take it all on. You may have to take on this role. Be brutal. Prioritization is your secret juice to make it to the finish line.

*　　*　　*

Okay, regardless of the whack-a-moles and constipated pythons, you have to get started. And, that is exactly what this book is about. Reboot. Reboot strategy and restart technology innovation to enable your company to compete.

It's possible, and it begins with you.

ABOUT THE AUTHORS

Lisa B. Jasper

Lisa is the co-founder and chairwoman of Thought Ensemble. Lisa has over fifteen years of consulting experience focused on the intersection of business organizations and technology, and as the coauthor of *Reboot: Competing With Technology Strategy,* she put her knowledge to work in book form. At the heart of *Reboot* is the notion that companies must reboot the way they think about IT organizations in the broader context of business strategy. Lisa's purpose for writing this book was to introduce a new way of thinking about technology as it relates to business strategy.

The compelling factors that drove Lisa to assist in the creation of Thought Ensemble were her love of consulting and thought leadership, but more importantly, the focus required for strategic planning in technology organizations in order for them to be successful. She believes focus is clearly the firm's differentiating ingredient and is grateful for the chance to do what she loves with colleagues and clients who challenge her to think more progressively every day. Her idea of fun is finding ways to ensure that great ideas don't end up on the shelf, and creating unique approaches to make those strategies actionable.

Her consulting career includes applications development and strategy roles with Accenture (Andersen Consulting), The Boston Consulting Group, Tactica Technology Group, Hitachi Consulting, and Pariveda Solutions. She has an MBA from Duke's Fuqua School of Business and a Computer Science degree from Trinity University.

Lisa currently serves on the board of the Denver Business Series and co-chairs the Colorado Software and Internet Association's Education Committee. She sits on the Colorado alumni board for Trinity University and Fuqua Business School. In her spare time, she loves to read, attend her book club, and participate in wine classes, golf, yoga, hiking, and skiing. She resides in beautiful Colorado with her husband and budding family.

Jim Smelley

Jim is co-founder and CEO of Thought Ensemble. With over fifteen years of experience providing technology and management consulting, Jim wanted to share insights on how companies can reboot their IT strategy, so he coauthored this transformational book, *Reboot: Competing With Technology Strategy*. At the heart of *Reboot* is the Strategy MAP, a comprehensive model that assists companies as they rethink their IT strategy to achieve competitive advantages.

Jim co-founded Thought Ensemble on a clear mission to focus on the strategic uses of technology in organizations, rather than to continue to perpetuate old ways of implementing technology. Jim has a fascination for the application of technology to solve business problems and specifically in leveraging emerging technologies to rethink business strategy. Despite taking strategy very seriously, he enjoys designing strategies with smart, engaged teams to such an extent that it could almost be considered a form of recreation.

Jim's consulting career includes technology and strategy roles at Pariveda Solutions, Hitachi Consulting, Experio Consulting, Tactica Technology Group, and Deloitte Consulting. He was formerly a developer and tester with IQ Software.

Jim currently serves on the Operations Committee of Big Thought and is a Big Brother with Big Brothers/Big Sisters. He has a B.S. in Computer Science from Trinity University and lives in Dallas, Texas.

ABOUT THE COMICS

After a combined thirty years of consulting, we've got a lot of stories to tell. However, it would be inappropriate to share actual tales related to our clients, and obviously they wouldn't appreciate it. So we created a cast of characters that allowed us to share some of the funniest things we've witnessed.

A wonderful artist named Jennifer Carter drew the comics. We couldn't be more pleased. Somehow her excellent drawings make these comics much funnier than they were when they were simply in textual form (maybe still not funny enough, but clearly much better). The two main characters are Pascal and Bernie. Pascal is a well-intentioned but completely ineffectual strategy guy. Bernie is a cranky, old-school bureaucrat.

Jim went on a mandatory no-Scott Adams and no-Bill Watterson hiatus while we were writing these comics, but considering he's read everything either of them has written (at least twice…and in the case of Watterson, mostly six or seven times), he's a little afraid that some of their humor might have snuck in. In fact, he's pretty sure he stole a rhyme from "Calvin and Hobbes" and some of the punch lines sound awfully similar to "Dilbert." We don't believe we've stolen anything outright, but there are some strong influences, so we would like to thank the artists who influenced us with their comedic genius. At any rate, we hope they have our own flavor and we hope you like them.

INDEX

A

alignment, 15–17

Altair 8800, 11

Amazon, 14

American Airlines, 9–10

analysis, 82–84

annual budget, 54–55

AOL, 14

Apple Computer, 11

Apple II, 11

Approach component, 33, 36–37, 40–43, 73–86

    combining with Model, 84–86

    hypothesis creation, 79–81

    overview of, 73–76

    problem definition, 76–78

    Project component and, 90

    tests and refinements, 81–84

assessment, 43, 44, 89, 90, 92–95

AT&T, 14

attachment, to ideas, 82

B

Balanced Scorecard, 32

Barnes and Noble, 14

BASIC, 10

BCG Matrix, 32

Box, George E., 49

brainstorming, 80–81

Britannica, 14

budget, 54–55

business

    adoption of email by, 12–14

    divide between IT and, 5–9, 15–18

early use of computers in, 9–12

Web and, 14–15

business culture, 65–67, 73

business management systems, 58–59

business models, 49

business objectives, 52

business processes, 61–63

business strategy, technology and, 1–2, 7–8, 15–18, 32–33, 51

C

capability gap, 67–68

change

enrolling others in, 108

resistance to, 100

cloud computing, 23–25

COBOL, 10

collaboration, 25–27

competitive advantage, 7, 8, 10

complexity, 56–58

computers

early, 9–11

PCs, 11–12

consumer adoption, of mobile technology, 22

corporate culture, 65–67, 73

cost containment, 61

cost reduction, 17–18, 52, 54–55

Craigslist, 14

critical thinking, 35

criticism, 80, 81, 82–84

culture clash, 65–67

customers

engagement by, 26

internal, 6, 7, 15, 17, 51–53

D

debate, 82–84

deliverables, 100

delivery method, 59–64

challenges, 60–63

process improvement and, 60–61

process rigidity and, 61–63

questions about, 60

dependencies, 71–72

Digital Equipment Corporation (DEC), 10

distractions, 63, 108–109

E

eBay, 14

economies of scale, 24

email, 12–14

execution, 35–36, 43, 98–102

F

failure

fear of, 73

of strategy, 98–100

falsifiability, 75

focus, 35

G

globalization, 7

goals, measurable, 79–80

Google, 14

H

hierarchies, 68–70

hypothesis creation, 42, 75, 79–81, 96–97

hypothesis testing, 42–43, 81–84

I

IBM, 9–10

idea generation, 80–81

ideas, attachment to, 82

information technology (IT)

See also IT organizations

divide between business and, 5–9, 15–18

history of, 9–15

investment decisions, 54–55

innovation, 2, 7, 73–74, 96

internal customers, 6, 7, 15, 17, 51–53

Internet

collaboration and sharing on, 25–27

email, 12–14

mobile devices and, 20–23

as platform, 23–25

World Wide Web, 14–15

iPad, 19

IT narcissism, 51–53

IT organizations, 12

cloud computing and, 25

creation of, 13–14

culture clash and, 65–67

divide between business and, 5–9, 14

internal focus of, 6, 7, 15, 17, 51–53

lack of respect for, 64

organization challenges, 65–70

running like businesses, 17–18, 51–53

structure of, 68–70

talent building in, 67–68

Trusted Advisor concept and, 16–17

iTunes, 14, 21

L

laws, scientific, 74–75

M

marketing, 26

measurable goals, 79–80

meetings, 13

memos, 12, 13

mental models, 38–39, 49

minicomputers, 10

mistakes, fear of, 73

mobile devices, 20–23

Model component, 33, 36–40, 49–72

    combining with Approach, 84–86

    delivery method, 59–63, 64

    organization, 64–70

    strategy, 49–55

    technology, 55–59

moving forward, 109–110

myopic solutions, 60–61

N

Napster, 14

O

organization

    challenges, 65–70

    in Model, 64–70

    questions about, 65

organizational hierarchy, 68–70

P

partially implemented systems, 57

Pauling, Linus, 80

personal computers (PCs), 11–12

plan, 43, 44, 45, 90, 98–101

Popper, Karl, 74–76

Porter's Five Forces, 32

prioritization, 110–111

problem definition, 41, 76–78

process improvement, 60–61

process "sacred cows", 61–63

productivity, 7

programming languages, 10

Project component, 33, 36–37, 43–45, 87–102

    Approach component and, 90

    assessment, 89, 90, 92–95

    overview of, 87–91

    plan, 90, 98–101

    scope, 91

    vision, 89, 90, 95–98

project plans, 88–89

public relations, 26

R

redundant systems, 57

risk avoidance, 73

risk management, 52

rogue system phenomenon, 57

S

SABRE (Semi-Automated Business Research Environment), 9–10

safety, 58–59

science, 2, 74–75

scope, project, 91

security, 13–14

sharing, 25–27

simplicity, 39, 45

small business

    competitive advantage of, 19, 24

    technological innovation and, 19–28

Smith, C.R., 9, 10

Software as a Service (SaaS), 23–24, 59

Sony, 14

speed, 19, 28, 74

standard processes, 61–63

start-ups

    See also small business

    competitive advantage of, 19

    Web-based collaboration and, 26–27

strategic initiatives, testing, 84

strategic role, of technology, 6–8, 12, 16

strategic thinking, 8, 12, 28, 32, 38–39, 44–45, 55, 73, 95
    See also strategy
strategy
    all-encompassing, 53–54
    barriers to defining and implementing, 105–111
    budget and, 54–55
    business, 1–2, 7–8, 15–18, 32–33, 51
    definition of, 51
    execution of, 98–102
    failures, 98–100
    in Model, 49–55
    questions about, 50–51
    technology, 50–55, 59–63
Strategy MAP, 2, 28
    Approach component, 33, 36–37, 40–43, 73–86
    Model component, 33, 36–40, 49–72
    overview of, 31–38, 46–47
    problems addressed by, 35–36
    Project component, 33, 36–37, 43–45, 87–102
structure, organizational, 68–70
SWOT, 32
system architecture, 56–58

T
tablets, 19
talent development, 67–68
technological innovations
    cloud computing, 23–25
    mobile devices, 20–23
technology
    advances in, 19–20
    business strategy and, 1–2, 7–8, 15–18, 32–33
    challenges, 56–59
    complexity of, 56–58
    delivery method for, 59–63
    history of, 9–15

    infrastructure, 56–58

    innovation and, 7

    investment decisions, 54–55

    in Model, 55–59

    questions about, 56

    safety issues, 58–59

    strategic role of, 6–8, 12

technology skills, 67–68

technology strategy, 32–34, 50–55

telephones, 12–13

tests, of hypothesis, 42–43, 81–84

Trusted Advisor concept, 16–17

U

universal laws, 74–75

utility computing, 24–25

V

vision, 43, 44, 45, 89, 90, 95–98

W

Web-based collaboration, 25–27

Web sites, 14–15

Wikipedia, 14

World Wide Web, 1, 14–15

Y

Yahoo!, 14